The First One Hundred Years

Poems, Prose, & Praise

By Melvin C. Young Sr.

Edited by Carla G. Harper

Veritas Conquistor Publishing
North Carolina

Copyright © 2017 by **Melvin C. Young Sr.** with **Veritas Conquistor Publishing.**

All rights reserved. No part of this publication may be reproduced, distributed or transmitted in any form or by any means, without prior written permission.

Printed in the United States of America.

Melvin C. Young/Carla G. Harper
P.O. 39436
Greensboro, NC 27438
www.carlagharper.com/mel-young/

Publisher's Note: This is a work of fiction. Names, characters, places, and incidents are a product of the author's imagination. Locales and public names are sometimes used for atmospheric purposes. Any resemblance to actual people, living or dead, or to businesses, companies, events, institutions, or locales is completely coincidental.

Book Layout © 2017 BookDesignTemplates.com

The First One Hundred Years: Poems, Prose, and Praise/ Melvin C. Young Sr., Edited by Carla G. Harper -- 1st ed.
ISBN 978-0-9971907-0-0

To Martha, my wife, who always smiled

Contents

Forward By Mel 5

Wisdom and Living 9

Faith 109

Remembering and History 145

Nature 235

About Mel 267

*All images of paintings are originals by Mel.

FORWARD BY MELVIN C. YOUNG

Over the last one hundred years, so many good things have happened to me.

I remember first experiencing God's presence as a small boy, lying in the soft grass near what we called "The Big Rock" by the Yadkin River. I looked up at the sky, and such a peaceful feeling overcame me. I felt so very happy. All my fears were removed. Everything seemed at peace in God's beautiful world. The sense of peace was so powerful that I drifted off to sleep.

God was in the stillness down by the river. Throughout my childhood, I found a sense of solitude by the river. I sometimes wish for that stillness again, that knowing God's presence, like I did down by the river so long ago.

My mama helped me write my first poem when I was about twelve-years-old, called *Down By The River*:

Down by the river, the sun is setting very low,
While the cool breezes blow.
Birds flying to their favorite limbs,
To sing their sweet little hymns.
And here by the Yadkin River,

I can sit by this shade tree,
And listen to their singing.

I read not long ago that poetry is healing. In school, I despised poetry, probably because I didn't understand it. I didn't really begin to write poetry or paint and carve wood until I became disabled in 1973. For some unknown reason, I wrote a few poems trying to express my feelings at that time. My family was very kind and encouraged me. Poetry and painting have helped me through many bad times. Both seemed to allow the emotions and feelings I was holding back to surface.

For years, I rang the church bell at the little brick church in Yadkin Mill Village. I was also the village paperboy. I was collecting one Saturday morning from Ray Simmerson, and he asked if I wanted a tip. I said, "Yes." And he said, "Stay away from wild women."

All my customers were friendly. Yadkin Mill Village was a very friendly, sharing community. A community isn't so much a locale as it is a state of mind. You find it in places where folks ask how you're doing because they care. A community also expects a lot from its members.

It's good when people expect a lot from you. Expectation is a blessing, not a curse. It's a beautiful thing when people expect something decent of you. It means you have given reason for confidence, like when John the Baptist was born, and his father sang a beautiful song about all the things his boy would do. Then the boy went out and did them. Many a powerful life has its start in expectation.

While working on my forestry merit badge as a Boy Scout, on the way to my Eagle Badge, I was told to not water trees too much because it would make for a shallow root system. Trees without a lot of water must grow deep roots in search of moisture. In a way that is true in our lives. I have always prayed that my children's lives would be easy, and I tried to make life easy for them.

I pray that my sons will grow deep roots so that they can draw strength from the hidden sources of God. Too many times we pray for ease, but that's a prayer seldom met. What we need to do is pray for roots that reach deep into God's eternal love so when the storms and winds blow, we won't be swept away.

I have my dark and sad days, but I have more sunshine than shadows, more hope that disappointments, more faith than despair. On my life's journey, I am still climbing from the dark valley to the light on the mountaintop.

There are three things I'd like to find up there. One is a cool spring like the one on our farm, another is an oak tree like the one on the Yadkin River that I used to climb, and third is the blood-red vine-ripened country tomatoes we grew way back when.

My heartfelt thanks go out to Carla Harper, who showed up in my life and said, "Let's publish your best work before you turn 100."

With Love,

Mel

WISDOM AND LIVING

MY LITTLE WILD ROSE

While hiking up the river one day,

I happened to spot a rose on my way.

I said, rose, why are you here in no-man's-land?

You're so beautiful, I don't understand.

You're hidden where you can't be found,

And you continue to bloom,

And give off your fragrant perfume.

My beautiful little wild rose,

Holding to your artistic pose,

Please tell me your sad story,

About your lonely life without glory.

When at your best, you are never seen,

Still standing straight, you never lean.

Your reasons for living are so few,

Why perform when no one can see you?

Why do you bother to show your beauty?
When no one can see you, why do your duty?
Why do you grow here in nature's backyard?
With no reward, where life is hard?

Your unseen charm is wasted here,
Without appreciation, don't you disappear?
Why hold your head so high each day,
When no one will ever pass your way?

You unfold your beauty without haste,
And all your perfection goes to waste.
Why in this wilderness do you grow?
Your sad story I'd like to know.

Tiny rose I'm beginning to believe,
Your sad tale has a lesson to teach.
It is not how far out you can reach,
Not the pride and glory that you take,

Not the great show that you can make,
Not who you are or where you live
That determines what you have to give.

It's being all you can with your little spark,
Even when no one is there and all is dark.
It's still doing your best when all alone,
Showing that the beauty of living must go on.

Your radiant beauty is always there to see,
It's the way our lives were meant to be.
Now little rose keep doing your thing.
To yourself and God, love you will bring.
If in your life time you have no fame,
Keep using your talents, never be ashamed.

Little wild rose when you wilt and die,
There is always someone by your side.
God is watching when everyone is gone.
You have a purpose so just bloom on.

Your story is no longer sad at the close.

You've taught me a lesson, Little Wild Rose.

*As a boy, I would hike up the river very often. Just before my 14th birthday in May of 1931, I hiked up the river and back through the woods. I saw a small wild rose shining bright in the sunshine. It was growing between two large rocks with very little soil to grow in. The next year, my 9th grade English teacher assigned a theme every Friday. We got to read them in class. I wrote one about the wild rose. I wish I had the theme that I turned in, but that was a long time ago. For many years in May, I'd hike up the Yadkin River to see my little wild rose. It seemed to never grow any taller, but it bloomed every year. In later years after I started trying to write a few poems, I remembered that wild rose and wrote what would become my favorite poem.

MY CHAPEL ON A HILL

On this bright frosty morning,
A bright new day is dawning.
I walk through a field
To my Little Chapel on a hill.

A silent place, I hold so dear,
A holy hush lingers here.
I feel the wind blowing free,
I marvel at the beauty I see.

My eyes find where the horizon ends,
Where the light blue begins.
This special morn' He seems so near.
I see His holy light shining clear.

Through a curtain of lifted haze,
Here God's universe can amaze.
The beauty of earth so divine,

With its colors so sublime.

I look past the rising sun,
Where the mountains meet the sea.
And I look at the simple things,
That only a loving God can bring.

My Chapel on this special hill,
Not a church but a holy place still.
A place for only God and me,
Where I find joy in being free.

Here the greatest cathedral of all,
Sends a message that He is Lord.
Echoing the sound of an alter call,
From this beauty within nature's walls.

This special morn' I worship here,
Upon earth's sacred holy sod.
For now, I'm free from pain and fear,

I am in the chapel of a holy God.

*A short ways up the river from our house in Yadkin on a hill overlooking the river – the same place where I found my little wild rose - were many rocks. I made a cross with rocks about the size of softballs at the top of the hill. I would kneel at the foot of this cross and pray most every morning. It was a holy place for me.

OLD AGE

I'm lucky. Now I'm getting old.

For me, it was quite a goal.

In life, I have paid my dues.

I have no reason to feel blue.

In my own and feeble way,

I have saved for this day.

Not money, silver or gold,

But many things that're very old.

Like a treasure of thoughts,

And memories I have brought.

I have done my very best,

I have earned a time to rest.

The best of all the things I've saved,

To have and enjoy at this stage

Is a new set of rules,

And a new set of sharp tools.

There's more in life to gain.
The joy out-weighs the pain.
I've had good times in the past,
My memories will make them last.

I'm still trying to make the rounds.
I plan to cover more grounds.
I won't need to drink a little toddy.
Bad habits hamper the body.

Age never hinders my will,
Life is a challenge still.
I will always think young,
And never think that I'm done.

The years, I'll never keep score,
I won't stop – I'll still do more.
I'll not act like old folks do.

They're lucky to get old too.

I'll never do what is wrong.
Happiness comes when sin is gone.
With the ever-rising morning sun,
For me, life has just begun.
Bad days I can count a few,
Many happy days I count too.
No matter what people may say,
I have surely had my day.

Time seems to go so fast,
And I can't change the past.
Even when life has been rotten,
With age, all is forgotten.

I know not where or when,
But this is not the end.
There surely is much more.
Old age can open another door.

It's the good life I still seek after.

I look forward to the hereafter.

My hope grows with his love,

Because it comes from God above.

BITTER WITH THE SWEET

Why ugliness before beauty?

Why excuses before duty?

Why a storm before a rainbow?

Why from dirt do flowers grow?

Dark skies first then the blue.

Sunshine above then sunset's rich hue.

We till the soil before the yield,

Harvest after working the fields.

Before we reap we must plow.

When giving thanks, we must bow.

Takes darkness to make light.

And calmness comes after fright.

Takes a night to make a day.

We are lost before we find our way.

First sorrow then gladness.

Joy will follow, after sadness.
Takes work to make our mark.
Takes toil before we embark.

Rain clouds to make flowers,
And minutes to make hours.
Smiles come after a baby cries.
Dark skies change when, dawns arise.

Darkness changes to a heavenly glow.
Light comes down to us here below.
Peace comes after a war is fought.
A high price but freedom is bought.

Life's advancement carrying many scars.
Still night-time has its sparkling stars.
Sometimes we pay a dear price,
By not being willing to sacrifice.

First the bitter then the sweet.

Takes both, to make life complete.

A fire starts with only a spark.

It makes shadows in the dark.

At the end, a better life resumes.

Now joy and beauty is in bloom.

Take the bitter with the sweet.

Then life we are willing to meet.

TOY BOX

The old toy box is still around,
Full of tops that were handed down.
The hinges covered with rust
Are all covered with memories and dust.
Tin soldiers with peeling paint,
A Jack-in-a-box ready for leaping.
A bounty of toys made by hand,
A little baby doll still sleeping.

A windup choo-choo ready to run.
Marbles, tops, and yo-yos for fun.
A tiny tea set and a checker game,
Even tinker-toys and blocks remain.

Some were slept with in trundle beds
Holding a doll while prayers were said.
They made young hearts lighter.
Made a dark night much brighter.

The old toy box is now dragged out.
Toys are ready to be scattered about.
From the attic, a cold, lonely place,
into eager hands in a wide-open space.
A new generation can rummage through
The funny old toys painted red and blue.
And play like children from other days,
Still giving love in so many ways.

How many times are they handed down,
Perhaps as long as children are around.
To come out again in this happy place,

To this old box overflowing with toys,
comes generations of girls and boys.
With contentment, I watch them play,
Memories come back in many ways,

TALENT

I have no voice for singing.

I cannot make a speech.

I have no gift for music.

I know I cannot teach.

I'd be no good at leading.

I cannot organize.

And anything I write,

Would never win a prize.

It seems my only talent

Is neither big nor rare.

Just to listen and encourage

And to fill a vacant chair,

But all the gifted people could not so brightly shine

Were it not for those who use

A talent such as mine.

REMINISCING AS I GROW OLDER

It seems like just a short time ago,

With peace of mind I started to grow.

I could hear music and church bells ringing.

I marveled at the blue skies and birds singing.

Many memories of lemonade, rainbows, and games.

A kind of happiness that's hard to explain.

Cracking walnuts in the shade of a tree,

Feeling a cool breeze and feeling free.

A bag of marbles and a kite of broom sedge,

Catching butterflies, keeping a rabbit in a cage.

Spinning tops, playing so many fun games.

Every new day full of joy and never the same.

A spring, a gourd dipper, tadpoles, how enchanted,

Beautiful flowers growing yet never planted.

Just living with beautiful roses and fresh air,

And knowing that with love God put them there.

WHAT IS LOVE?

What is the meaning of love, today?

Is it just a word some people say?

Is it a feeling deep down within?

Or is it words you say now and then?

Is it felt in music that is so sweet?

Can it be in our hearts when we weep?

Is it felt in an old man's heart?

Can it be love playing her part?

Does love only live in our youth?

Will love come if we seek the truth?

Can it be a feeling on a special day?

Is it believing everything people say?

Is it true love that comes from mom and dad?

Is it happiness or a tear when sad?

Do you feel love when you are alone?

Does it come from a source unknown?

Is love what keeps you from being blue?
Is love someone you depend on that is true?
Is love someone who will take the time
To listen and show you some mind?

The mystery of love may never be solved.
To understand love, you must get involved.
So, trust in love, then you can sing,
"Falling in love is the natural thing."

DARK BEFORE THE LIGHT

First the dark, then the light.
A morning bright after the night.
A morning star, the night must go,
First dark clouds then a rainbow.

Before a sparkling dawn can rise,
The sun must clear the cloudy skies.
Life can have many fears,
But later joy and laughter will appear.

Dark before the light, a constant theme,
A nightmare, like a phantom's dream.
Many tears, life is sometimes sad,
Then comes truth to make us glad.

We pay a dear price for our sadness,
Soon a morning we wake with gladness.
We find the true light shining bright,

Brought forward by the resurrection-light.

With our fears, a midnight vigil keep,

Yet with God's love we can sleep.

Far behind us a dense darkness spread,

Then a path appears where angels tread.

No need to linger where darkness forms,

With truth, we are above the storms.

I hope for you an end with love and joy, no fear,

No pain, just a smile without a tear.

CARVING A BOY

I've carved totem-poles and Indian heads.
Now I'll carve a boy instead.
I'll carefully carve my kind of boy,
And mold him with a smile of joy.

It will keep me busy the long day through,
Just teaching him the truth and what to do.
I'll make him honest, brave and true.
With laughter, he'll never be blue.

It won't be easy, it's part uphill.
He'll get to the top with his strong will.
He may twist and turn and give a sigh,
But he'll move on even if the mountain is high.

When the going is rough, he won't turn about.
He'll never give up, he'll stick it out.
Life's uphill climb may be very slow,

And it seems he can't take another blow,

But he won't give up when he's hardest hit,
For this is the time when he mustn't quit.
To him, to become a strong man seems afar,
I'll say, 'You don't know how close you are.
I'll carve you into a real strong man,
And on your two feet proudly you will stand.

I've finished and now it's time to depart,
Carving you has helped me find my heart.
We've shared your youth, now you're grown.
Passing time can change it not; you're on your own.

Now I think did I make him a lovely lad?
Did having me shape him make him glad?
Making him into a man did I leave out a tiny part?
Did I give him self-esteem and a loving heart?

I tried to carve in less about the love of power,

And more about the importance of each hour.

In my mind with all my love, I must not forget,

That he's just a boy and not a man yet.

Now my carving is done. He leaves my hand,

He's on his own to follow God's command.

OLD AGE CAN CHANGE US

From my recliner, now old and infirm, I can see there are needs all around my community. Old age changes our health and mobility. We can't do the things we use to do when we were younger. But we need to live in the present not in the past. We can still live an enthusiastic life and take advantage of some of the new inventions.

God can use you and me. He always uses common people to make an uncommon difference. I believe fulfillment is discovering one thing you love to do and then doing it with all your heart for Jesus Christ.

Aging can bring wisdom and humility, or we can let it make us prideful and stubborn. Age imposes limits to this life, but we know that another life in heaven awaits those who belong to Jesus Christ.

I believe that God has given us the skills to meet every need, if we'll let God be in control of our lives. I often pray, "Lord, use me, show me what to do."

Don't use old age as an excuse, let it be one more leg on the journey of your life.

What is your talent? Are you using it?

SUCCESS OR FAILURE

The father of our country, George Washington, lost two-thirds of the battles he fought in the Revolutionary War, but he won the War and helped found a great nation. Babe Ruth, the great baseball slugger, hit 714 home runs, but he struck-out 1,339 times. He's the most famous player and was a big attraction.

After Thomas Edison had experimented 10,000 times with his storage battery and still could not get it working, a friend tried to comfort him. Edison said, "Why, I have not failed. I have just found 10,000 ways that won't work." Edison patented more than 1,000 inventions. Who could call him a failure?

A faithful old preacher felt he had failed when one year only a boy was added to his congregation. That boy went on to become a missionary. He brought the gospel to a people that had never heard the gospel of Jesus Christ.

If life's journey has put you in a ditch, take heart. Pull yourself out. Success is just ahead.

The world will measure us on success. But God will measure us by our faithfulness and courage to keep on keeping on.

LET US GO ON A JOURNEY TOGETHER

When I was just a boy, I heard a soft voice in my heart say, "Let us go on a journey together."

I followed the voice. At first, the nights were crystal clear and the sky displayed a million stars. I was not afraid. We sang songs of ages long since passed.

Then a fog settled over the night and the stars were lost behind dark clouds. I found myself in a dark valley. Other voices called out, "Come, go with us on our way, it's a good way." I started to go with them.

Then I saw a dim light through the fog. I turned away from them to follow my first guide. The fog lifted and I saw a bright sunrise. The small, soft voice spoke to me again. "When you journey with me, you must journey alone for a time. Until you have made this journey alone with me, you are not ready to guide others along the way."

I felt at peace and knew it was the spirit of God teaching me.

Later, the soft voice came again, saying, "Come with me, let us go on a journey together to the mountain heights where we will always be together, and you will know me better."

From the mountaintop, I saw in a new way through God's eyes with help from my spirit guide. "Now you are ready to start others on the same journey. You can teach them that the mountaintop lies just ahead with all its beauty, but they must choose to leave the dark valley with only the light of Jesus to follow," the soft voice said.

The journey can be short or long. Mine is now going on one-hundred years. This I do know, the journey is made of many little steps, most of which are overcoming our faults and growing in love for those traveling the journey with us.

ANOTHER ONE OF MY LOVE POEMS

Love is a beautiful experience. It is a way of life.

Love is when two hearts pledge as husband and wife.

Love is in our hearts, it grows each day.

If love is there during the good and bad it will stay.

Love is like a rose, it far outweighs

The pain of any thorn along life's way.

Love is a way of life made up of rain and sun.

Love is when two hearts have blended into one.

After so many years we still celebrate each day.

We share our affection but don't put them on display.

Each year a poem for you I'll write

To show my love for you with delight.

I'll write about your love and tender heart.

And how your smile drew me to you from the start.

We walked life's journey arm in arm.

Your sweet smile has been like a charm.

I love you more and more each day,

I guess that's all I need to say.

AN OLD VALENTINE

When you grow old, Valentine's Day is a special day.

I look through some old stuff packed away.

I think of old friends I'd still like to meet.

I think of old times; my heart skips a beat.

I find a Valentine made from paper about to fall apart.

It's yellow from age with dull red hearts.

The writing is dim, but it brought a smile to my face,

With it's pasted-on white lace.

A short note handwritten with care,

And a faded ribbon here and there.

It must have been a Valentine from my sweetheart.

Now, it's just a piece of paper falling apart.

I treasure this old homemade Valentine.

How happy I've been since you became mine.

RECIPE FOR A VITAL MARRIAGE

Begin with care, love, friendship, passion, and respect as your base ingredients. Blend in lots of understanding and forgiveness.

Bake continuously in the oven of commitment and trust.

Baste often and liberally with a sense of humor.

Serve with plenty of communication in a problem-solving atmosphere.

This is a tricky recipe that requires careful attention and the participation of two cooks. When it falls flat, check all ingredients and increase amounts as needed.

Prepare often for best results.

WITH LOVE

Life and love is a gift from God set before you.

To live it you must be true.

With love, you can endure strife.

For love is the energy of life.

Open your heart to love each day,
Then happiness will come your way.

A loving life you must seek,

If it's true love you want to keep.

What's worse than getting old?

No love from a single soul,

Or living only with your fears,

Missing out on love in later years.

Knowing that someone loves me,

Is a thought that sets me free.

Love can heal your sorrows.

With love, you look forward to many tomorrows.

With patience, love will endure.
With God's love, you can be secure.
For true love suffers long,
Loving others you can't go wrong.

Humility is love for others,
Treating them like brothers.
Selfishness is not loves way.
It is kind words that you say.

Like grace, love comes from above.
It's great to be in love.

THE MAN THAT IS TWELVE YEARS OLD

I know a man who lives in the land called everywhere.

You may not think he's a man by the close he wears.

Under that old coat lies a heart more precious than gold.

It's a man who's twelve years old.

You never can tell on what future street

That careless lad you might meet.

For many a Congressman is doing the chores,

And presidents once worked in lowly stores.

The hands that are busy with playthings now,

The rein of power will hold.

So, take off your hat and proudly salute,

The man who is twelve years old.

WHAT MADE A YOUNG BOY SMILE

Up the river banks so steep,

Where the pools are clear and deep.

Where the cat fish lies asleep,

Up the river and over the hills,

That's the place I want to be.

Just my best friend and me.

Together we love to play,

In the barn-loft among the hay.

Later tracing a homeward bee

To its honey that's all free.

Finding walnuts my friend and me,

Cracking them under a sycamore tree.

Up the river feeling free,

That's the life for my friend and me.

The fun and friendship was worthwhile.

Thinking of the joy we had, I just smile.

AS I GET OLDER

Sometimes it's hard to understand
Why I need a helping hand.
Often, I strain to catch what they say
Because I forgot my hearing aid.
I need people with cheerful smiles,
Friends who'll stop and chat for a while.

I don't like to hear them to say,
"You've told me that twice today."
I like people who know the way
To bring back memories of yesterday.

I love the ones who ease my days
In their loving ways.
I'd not change things if I could,
For now, I know that God is good.

LEGACY

Did I make a difference?

Did I make the world a little better?

Did I help someone live a better life?

Did I help fellow travelers find the right path?

Did I use my talents to help others?

At this old age, I wonder, have I wasted my time? Am I too old to think I can do more? I guess I'll keep on doing what I've been doing if God offers me abundant opportunities right where I am.

I can leave a legacy and hand down an example of the good life to this next generation. Yes, I wonder what my legacy will be. God is the answer to all my questions. God is good and loving. He is all powerful and has a purpose and a plan for you and me. He is in control of everything. Let him be in control of your legacy.

I LOVE THE MORNING

I love the mornings with my coffee cup,
Watching the sun as it is coming up.
From my porch, I see a flash of red.
It's the early bird cocking his head.

It's so quiet as the new day begins.
Earth's awaking stirs me from within.
Shadows start to move across the hills,
And yellow daises light up the fields.

The beauty of nature no longer concealed,
Sparkling dewdrops scattered across the fields.
Seeing the first sign of the morning light,
A new beginning at dawn, what a delight.

MY BOYS

That's my boy with the shining eyes.
He's the one chasing butterflies.
He's suntanned with wind-blown hair,
And loves the outdoors and fresh air.

He's always laughing, being good,
Or finding a trail through a pathless wood.
He'll swim the river around the bend,
And search for gold at the rainbow's end.

He can run very fast in all his races.
He loves the mountains and high places.
He hangs over the edge to see the view.
I know these precious days are few.

We're proud that he's a good Scout,
He's prepared and able when we campout.
Maybe they'll have great things to tell.

But I know they'll do the small things well.

Now it may seem like a very tiny part,
But sharing and loving is a work of art.
Soon they'll be men as childhood departs.
I hope we've helped to shape well their hearts.

FAMILY LIFE

Untied shoes with dangling lace,
Shirttail out, a dirty face.
Finding butterflies, worms and bugs,
And mud puddles, rocks and slugs.

Games and a tree to climb,
Always willing to earn a dime.
Boys with Grandpa grabbing a pole,
Heading for our fishing hole.
He's just a boy, a great kid.
Grandpa loves him as he is.

Children playing on the floor,
Another one hiding behind a door.
On the stairs a boy is playing,
A little one with a toy, just waiting.
Children in the yard pitching ball.
A little girl jumping in the hall.

Men are watching a football game

But Grandpa sleeps just the same.

Happy with the blessings God has sent

With his family together, he's content.

FEARFUL PLEASURES OF A TEN-YEAR-OLD BOY

Fears of youth are now turned to pleasures,

Ghost tales become a source of treasures.

Memories of long evenings by the fireside,

Scary stories told in the embers glow still abide.

Fearful pleasures, strange sights and sounds,

By this dying fireside many fears are found.

Terror of going out after dark with no light,

Dark ghostly shadows causing my fright.

With mixed feelings, I heard tales of a ghost,

A galloping headless horseman my only host.

Fearful evil spirits in my thoughts,

What fear they brought.

Hearing tales of witchcraft in a dark field.

Fighting dragons with sword and shield.

Ghost houses, graveyards, a haunted bridge,
Demons from outer space on a phantom ridge.

I could hear ghosts and see their ugly scars,
From the fire came comets and shooting stars.
Light from a distant window gave a dim glow,
Casting rays of trembling light across the snow.

Shaking with fear from the smallest sound,
Afraid of the howling wind blowing all around.
Froze with terror, dreading to open my eyes,
To see the horror of phantoms lighting up the skies.

I'm safe if I avoid graveyards and black cats.
I never walk under a ladder or enter a cave with bats.
A horseshoe or a gray mule can keep ghosts away.
Breaking a mirror means bad luck, seven years and a day.

No evil can come if there's a horseshoe clothed in red.
Ward away ghosts when it's hung over a bed.

For luck, I'll carry a pinch of salt and a buckeye

And count every buzzard in the sky.

FELLOWSHIP

When a fellow hasn't got a cent, feeling kinda blue,
And clouds hang thick and won't let the sunshine thru.
It's a great thing, oh my brethren, for a fellow just to lay
His hand upon your shoulder in a friendly sort of way.

It makes a man feel odd; it makes the tear drops start.
And you kinda feel a flutter in a region of your heart.
You can't meet his eyes; you don't know what to say
When a hand is on your shoulder in a friendly way.

This world's a curious compound with its honey and gall,
Its cares and bitter crosses, but a good world after all.
A good God made it; leastwise, that is what I say,
When a hand is on your shoulder in a friendly way.

YOU HAVE A CHOICE

Why live in this artificial slumber,
Knowing that your days are numbered.
The wonders of life you always neglect.
Putting up a good front so no-one will suspect
That you're thinking you're not fit,
Not willing to start and ready to quit.

From your sorrows, you can have relief.
You can start anew without old grief.
You must stand tall, like an oak tree.
Then you'll see how much better life can be.
Learn to live and love with God as your guide.
He will hold your hand and be by your side.

You can start a happy new day
With your old footprints washed away.
Like a high tide sweeps the shore,
You can hear music in the ocean's roar.

You can wipe out your evil thoughts,
And a new way of life can be taught.

When the light seems so dim,
It's never dark enough to lose sight of him.
Life is sometimes hard for you and me.
The song of life is full of mystery.
Like fields of bright golden daffodils,
Soon to whiten and blow across the hills.

We all have a job to do, 'tis true.
No matter how small it may seem to you.
He has a plan, it's up to you to choose,
Right or wrong, win or lose.

He's with you always; he becomes a part.
The choice is easy with love in your heart.

FISHING WITH MEMORIES

I think I'm wise, have a scheme,

Pretend to fish, instead I dream.

My dreams take me far away

Into streams of yesterday.

On the river where dreams hold sway,

Where the big fish never gets away.

Remembering the big snow so white,

Bringing much pleasure and delight.

With cold hands and cheeks aglow,

Making snow angels in the snow.

A winter wonderland here below.

How fast flows the current of time,

As memories of youth tugs at my line.

On the Yadkin where I used to play,

Even if the big ones got away.

Drifting in the current of my youth,

In dreams now I have found the truth.

Here I find peace and all is fine.

The fish of life tugs at my line.

I make my play too late, I'm afraid.

All the big ones got away.

WHY I WRITE POEMS

I fashion my poems from my heart.
My memories play a big part.

Like the rhythm from the rain,
With poetry life goes on without pain.
I see the beautiful green hills,
As I tread through the open fields.

With my guardian angel leading the way,
I say goodbye to skies of gray.
A forest door is open wide.
The beautiful landscape welcomes me inside.

Happy thoughts keep me warm in the night.
Then poems come to me when it's light.
As I write, I see angels in the sky,
And blue birds as they fly.

I can smell the wild rose as I write.

All this makes my life so bright.

Each day I start anew.

Each day God gives me a new view.

Poems come from my heart, from inside.

When I write, the door of my heart is open wide.

I'M OBSOLETE

I never could admit defeat,

But now it's clear, I'm obsolete.

When I hear someone say," DOTCOM,"

I don't know where they're coming from.

A mystery that I still don't get,

Is what and where is the internet?

When my wife said, she has a mouse,

I said, well, fumigate the house.

Am I the only living male

Who doesn't understand email?

I always vote and pay my taxes,

But I'm not sure just what a fax is.

Nor do I quite know what it means,

When people go to church in jeans.

It doesn't matter what we wear,

The main thing is that we are there.

Sometimes I must tell myself,

You're old, you belong on the shelf!

But really, that's not so hard to bear.

I'm obsolete, and I don't care.

THINGS THAT MAKE THIS OLD MAN FEEL GOOD

Thinking about the first time I fell in love.

A hot shower once in a while.

Laughing so hard that I cry.

Getting EMAIL.

Taking a drive by our old home place.

Playing my old favorite songs.

Watching it snow.

Eating Bar-B-Que.

Winning a competitive game of cards.

Having friends bring me a cake.

Spending time with close friends.

Hearing my family laugh.

Watching a sunset or a sunrise.

Getting out of bed early in the morning and going to my computer.

Going to the beach.

Laughing at myself.

Eating chocolate candy.

Remembering Mama's Coke bottle with the holes punched through the cap to sprinkle clothes with water while she ironed with a flat iron.reaming of home milk delivery in glass bottles with cardboard stoppers, and I saved the stoppers to use as play money.

Remembering the fun we had talking on the party line phone. Reminiscing about what we got with S&H green stamps and how good the food was from an ice box.

LET'S GO BACK TO A TIME WHEN

Let's go back to when vacation was all summer long.

Decisions were made by going "Eent-meeny-miney-mo."

Mistakes corrected by simply exclaiming, "Do it over."

Race issue meant arguing about who ran the fastest.

Money issues were handled by whoever was the banker in "Monopoly."

Catching fireflies happily occupied an entire evening.

It was unbelievable that dodge-ball wasn't an Olympic event.

Having a weapon in school meant being caught with a slingshot.

Scrapes and bruises were kissed and made better by Mom.

Taking drugs meant orange-flavored chewable aspirin or a B.C. headache powder.

A BOY

A baby is weaned to become a boy,
Causing some sorrow and much joy.
All boys have the same creed.
Yet, each boy has different needs.
They want to enjoy every day.
They need love in a special way.

Boys climb into, on top and underneath,
Making noise like thunder thinking it's neat.
It's hard to put him to bed at night,
He fights when you turn off the light.

From girls, he will never take a dare.
Sometimes he puts bubble gum in their hair.
Boys are hated by most little girls,
Because boys, sometimes yank their curls.

Boys seem to always have a dirty face.

They stand ready always to run a race.

They have great energy, a big appetite,

Imagination, and enthusiasm for a fight.

A boy is not much for Sunday school,

And dislikes barbers and bedtime rules.

He likes Christmas toys and to day dream,

Knives, guns, and chocolate ice cream.

Boys like fire engines, tractors, trains,

Comic books, TV, and running in the rain.

They love frogs, dogs, and climbing trees.

They love the ocean and a strong breeze.

Crammed in his pocket you'll find a toy car,

An empty sack and a half-eaten candy bar.

A sling shot, two cents, and a code ring,

A worm, a rusty knife, and a piece of string.

There's more; a rock, a rope, four jelly beans.

All this, in the pockets of his cutoff jeans.

This magical creature with a freckled-face,

This boy is our hope for the future's race.

Now for overcoats and neckties he is shy,

And you will never know when he cries.

You can lock him out of your workshop,

But you can't lock him out of your heart.

When you walk, he tags along behind,

And you can't get him off your mind.

He's your son and thinks you're grand,

He's your master when he holds your hand.

When you are without hope and feeling sad,

He'll lasso your heart by saying, "Hi Dad."

He mends your shattered dreams by giving hope.

You can see his eyes saying," Dad, you can cope."

Boys cause grief, embarrassment, and delight,

They cause joy, making our future bright.

You're a king when he climbs on your knee,

And whispers, "Dad I love you, do you love me?"

A GOOD DAD

I love my dad; he's strong and true.

He teaches me the right things to do.

When I'm with Dad it's a lot of fun.

He helps me with projects I've begun.

He works all day 'til very late,

Gives thanks before passing our plates.

My eyes are watching him night and day.

I take in every word that he may say.

I've never seen him do anything that's bad,

I plan someday to be just like Dad.

I think he is the wisest of the wise,

No doubts about my dad will ever rise.

When I grow up, I will always be glad,

To follow his steps and be like Dad.

I believe that Dad is always right,

I depend on him to make my day bright.

I'll never use language of the street.

Dad's prayers and blessings, I'll repeat.

I'm waiting to grow up and be a man,

And set an example like dad, if I can.

I'll always remember my dad, you see,

For he has always done things with me.

A better Dad than mine you'll never find.

Every little boy needs a good Dad like mine.

A TIME FOR ROAMING

When I was a child I could dream all day.

I'd go deep into the woods and get far away.

Where troubles and trials are far and few.

My young life was good and all things new.

Youth is for carefree living, I do agree,

A time for roaming, like a river flowing free.

An age for learning with a yearning in my heart,

Life's an adventure, a mystery and I'm a part.

At sunrise, I wander down to my favorite spot,

Down a steep hill to the big rock.

I lay on its top dreaming and make-believe.

Looking up, I see the sky through birch leaves.

I'm living in a world of magic, happy as can be.

Knowing the big oak trees are watching over me.

The blue clouds are drifting and rolling above,

Nature's beauty, giving a feeling of peace and love.

I feel her strength as her arms embrace me.

With hugs from branches of a weeping willow tree.

A dream world I enter with wonder and new sight.

Overhead a blue bird flaps its wings in flight.

In a bush a rusty brown thrush builds a nest.

Loud is the chirp of crickets, disturbing my rest.

Hearing the flow of water rippling over a stone,

I see the beauty of a proud butterfly. I'm not alone.

I skip a rock across the water, the silence is broken.

From the swamp a catbird screams, a warning is spoken.

Echoes from the catbird's call, lingers over the stream.

While flowers nod to me and me to them as in a dream.

Nearby many birds come to feast in a mulberry tree.

They share with squirrels, they are all free.

Down the river, I sail a ship made from birch bark.

In the distance, I hear the song of a meadowlark.

I follow the ship downstream around the big rock.

For more boats, I use driftwood and pine bark.

Here on the big rock it's like a colored picture book.

I see the green forest and a clear shady brook.

From the earth a spring, like a fountain flows.

Here spring lizards, crawfish, and tadpoles grow.

A DROPPING OFF PLACE

I wish I could find a good place

To leave my mistakes and heartaches.

I'd drop my selfish greed and petty pain,

And change my life and start again.

I'd like to meet a friend along the trail,

To show the right way, so I'd not fail.

And help me do good things I've intended to do,

Like love of family and being true.

Somewhere on the trail there must be a place,

To drop my troubles and laugh away hate.

I need a new beginning, a new start.

I must keep on doing my part and have heart.

With a new start I'll do my best,

My anger and temper I'll put to rest.

I know there's some good in all of us,

Helping others without pay, that's a must.

With a helping hand I'll enjoy what I see,

For helping others, I'll be helping me.

Now I need no place to drop my sorrows,

I'm on the right path for tomorrow.

MY GRANDFATHER CHARLES CLEMENT

It takes time for a good life to mold.

Granddad is lucky to be getting old,

With his happy memories of the past,

They are good memories that will last.

Some people may forget, but still,

Granddad has done more good than ill.

These many years have made him wise,

He has made things right before he dies.

Now Granddad waits and wonders,

Counting the days by numbers.

But he never seems to fret,

And with not a touch of regret.

He can withstand all the grief,

Realizing life is so brief.

Memories like a glowing flame,
When happiness was his only aim.
Those memories will last forever more,
They can open many doors.

He's ready, this granddad is getting old,
But his hands are not ready to fold.
He keeps calm, there's no time rush,
Even when he hears the lonesome hush.
Someday his heart will cease to beat,
He's ready to kneel at his Makers feet,
The gates are open to let him in.
It's the beginning that has no end.

WALKING DOWN BY THE RIVER

This morning the crisp cool breeze reminds me of my youth, when I walked down to the river almost every morning. Each day was a new beginning for me filled with anticipation of excitement and fun. On the way to the river, I'd pass our clear cool spring decorated with green native ferns.

The old spring house, or trough as we called it, stood with a low swinging door on its rusty hinges. The spring water running through this trough kept everything cool. I'd stop to take a drink of sweet milk out of a gourd dipper. The milk was waiting for the cream to rise to the top to make butter. There was always a crock of buttermilk and mounds of butter at our house.

From there, I'd follow the small stream down to the river in search of our fish baskets. Fish caught would be placed into our fish box that was tied to a stump. Then I'd walk up and down the banks of the Yadkin River. Sometimes

I'd get there in time to see the awesome beauty of a sunrise over the river. The work of God in the stillness of the morning, painting the beautiful sunrise was then and still is the most beautiful, picture-perfect sight that I have ever seen.

I often thought about Jesus. Thinking back, I always felt close to him when I was alone by the riverside. It seems that I could feel his presence as I walked.

In the stillness of every morning I give thanks for the awesome beauty of His creation. I feel close to Him now just like I did back then, walking the banks of the Yadkin River with God and nature. I felt His magic. Nature is the art of God. I have never been happier, more at peace, and more aware of the beauty of his universe than when I'd go down to the riverside.

BEATITUDES FOR A FRIEND TO THE AGED

Blessed are they who understand

My faltered step and palsied hand.

Blessed are they who know that my ear today

Must strain to catch the things they say.

Blessed are they who seem to know

That my eyes are dim and my wits are slow.

Blessed are they who looked away

When coffee spilled at the table today.

Blessed are they with a cheery smile

Who stop to chat for a while.

Blessed are they who never say,

"You've told me that story twice today."

Blessed are they who know the way

To bring back memories of yesterday.

Blessed are they who make it known

That I'm loved, respected, and not alone.

Blessed are they who ease the days

On my journey home in loving ways.

YOUNG BOY AND OLD MAN

"Sometimes I drop my spoon," said the boy.

"I do that too," said the old man.

The little boy whispered, "I wet my pants."

"I do too," laughed the old man.

"I often cry," said the boy.

The old man said, "So do I."

"But worse of all," said the little boy,

"It seems grown-ups don't pay attention to me."

He felt the warmth of a wrinkled old hand,

"I know what you mean," said the little old man.

CONTENTMENT

I'm contented in my old rocking chair,

With friends ever ready to care.

I gaze out my window to see God's splendor.

Roses are blooming, each one a Blue-Ribbon contender.

From an acorn, I watched grow this huge oak tree.

Only with God could this be, no one's as powerful as he.

With God, loneliness turns into a song,

Night turns into day and sadness is gone.

The work of nature sets my spirit free.

It's another blessing God has sent to me.

Life is more beautiful as I grow older,

Like the seasons bringing yellow and gold.

The wonders of nature always there to behold,

Like a godly pattern just waiting to unfold.

Humbly, I often offer my praise,

For a rose, a friend and the joy of this day.

My life is revived and rekindled without pain.

It's a feeling of love like soft gentle rain.

HOLD HANDS

As years go by and heads turn gray,
Hold hands with those that are here today.
Give hugs when life's fires burn low.
Don't wait too long. We all must go.

We must give our love while we live.
To give this love, we must forgive.
Hold hands for the good life we seek.
Offer a hand to the old and to the weak.

SMILES

Smiles are like two-for-one coupons. Each time you let a smile spread across your lips, you light up the face and heart of someone else. Sooner or later a smile will come back around to you, just when you need it most.

No matter what you wear, the expression on your face is your greatest asset or liability. Don't wear your anger or hurt on your face with a frown. Trade that frown for a smile. Smiles go a long way toward making new friends – Give it a try!

Smiles come easier when you stay connected to good people and seek out things that bring you joy. Smiles attract warm welcomes. The happier you are to see others, the happier they'll be to see you.

Circumstances or people can take away your material possessions, your money, and your health. But no one can ever take away your precious memories. So, don't forget to make time to take opportunities to make memories every day. Then when you get old, it will be easier to smile as you remember.

SHE ALWAYS SMILED

I saw her smile throughout the years

When there should have been tears.

She did her work with a smile every day,

Whether good times or bad, that was her way.

For seventy years, we loved and cared for each other.

Four times she became a smiling mother.

We buried our dear daughter, a day of grief,

But she smiled with courage beyond belief.

Despite growing old, she still smiled and loved everyone.

Her work here on earth was almost done.

She left much beauty for all to see,

And memories of love that she shared with me.

Then came the end of her happy life's story,

As she went home to glory.

God sent a special angel to lead her away

On that special homecoming day.

And she smiled, her baby was waiting at heaven's door.

She held her in her arms, not waiting any more.

Forgive me now if I shed a tear,

I've missed her now for too many a year

I miss most her sweet smile,

But I'll see it again in a little while.

IT'S UP TO YOU

Not other's causing you trouble.

Not other's busting your bubble.

Not other's making you blue.

Not other's foiling you.

If success you can't find,

It's not others causing you to be behind.

It's up to you.

If you want a life that's right,

If you want your life to be a delight,

If you want good things in life,

Without too much strife,

It's up to you.

No need to turn to drinking,

You can change your way of thinking.

Stop traveling with the wrong clan,

If you want a good life have a plan.

It's up to you.

You can develop a desire for good things,

Seek out faith, peace it brings.

Now work your plan it's the thing to do,

Have determination to follow through.

Run your race, get into high gear.

Never allow negative thinking or fear.

If its hard work you dread,

You'll never get ahead.

You must have a real desire for success.

To succeed you must do your best.

It's up to you.

THE LISTENER

His thoughts, he kept mostly to himself.

His words were few, and never formed to glisten

He was a joy to all his friends.

You should have heard him listen.

DO YOUR BEST

A hero is the man who does what he can.

On life's journey, just do your best.

After that, you'll still have time to rest.

When troubles weigh you down like stones,

You've got to work to hold your own.

What you are called to makes up your final score,

Nothing less and nothing more.

Like it or not this is the race you are in.

With your handicap, you may not always win.

But still give it your best from the start,

That's what God calls your part.

And never forget kindness, no matter how small.

This is the love language of all.

THE LIGHTED CROSS AT LAKE JUNALUSKA

With winter comes the dark cold nights. I'm reminded of the darkness in this world and that God's light has overcome that darkness. "In him was life, and the life was the light of men" (John 1:4).

At times, I'm bombarded with sickness and a lot of negative thoughts and sorrow. If I allow myself to remember his words, I walk through the darkness with confidence, knowing that the path of life is lighted by the Lord's light.

I remember too that in the Blue Ridge Mountains of North Carolina, at the Methodist Assembly Grounds on Lake Junaluska burns a huge electric cross. For over one hundred years it has sent a gleaming light across the rugged hills. For many years, the Methodists only kept the cross lit during the summer season.

In 1922 that changed thanks to Southern Railroad engineers.

The Southern railroad tracks passed by that old burning cross. It became a beacon to those men at the throttle of those big engines. In a petition to the Methodists, they stated that the brilliantly lighted cross was a reminder of their responsibility, and of their sense of loyalty and fidelity to duty.

The Methodists granted their request and began keeping that large and unique symbol of the Cross of Calvary burning nightly throughout the year. Today, the cross still sends rays of light and hope across the mountainside overlooking beautiful Lake Junaluska to the train engineers as well as hundreds of thousands of travelers as they pass by year after year.

HOPE FOR THE JOURNEY

Before the mountaintop, there are many hills to climb.

Many disappointments, sweat and grime.

You'll know storms and burning heat.

Every man has loneliness he must meet.

In your heart, keep a happy song.

In hard times, it'll make you strong.

Don't travel with the bad crowd at all.

Those are the ones that'll surely make you fall.

At times, you'll be sick at heart.

You'll think the world is falling apart.

Have faith, God is willing to share.

He'll help you with the troubles you bear.

With God's helping, healing hand,

You'll always be able to take a stand.

Hang on; you can cope.

When you travel with Christ, there's always hope.

I'VE SEEN MANY A GREAT THING

I've seen water rippling down a stream.

I've gazed on daisies that seemed to gleam.

I've felt raindrops and snowflakes too.

I've marveled at rainbows in a sky of blue.

I've been on the river as a storm draws near.

I've watched it rage without any fear.

I've played ballgames with friends all day long.

I remember each one, they are all now gone.

I've camped in the mountains, hiking for miles.

I've searched out the sunset because it made me smile.

I've seen the golden moon slip slowly out of view.

I've awakened in the morning to cool morning dew.

I've felt the breeze blowing gently and so mild.

I've remembered all this from when I was a child

God created all this beauty; I know it's true.

And he created me, and he created you.

BOY SCOUT WISDOM

Once while as a Scout Master, I was teaching my Scouts about survival in the desert. I asked, "What are the three most important things you should bring with you in case you get lost in a desert?"

Several hands went up, and many important things were suggested such as food, matches, etc. Then one little boy eagerly raised his hand. "Yes Tommy, what are the three most important things you would bring with you?"

Tommy replied, "A compass, a canteen of water, and a deck of cards."

I asked, "Why That, Tommy?"

"Well," he answered, "The compass is to find the right direction, the water is to prevent dehydration."

"What about the deck of cards?",

"Well Sir, as soon as you start playing Solitaire, someone is bound to come up behind you and say, 'Put that red nine on top of that black ten.'"

FAITH

GOD OF LITTLE THINGS

He clothes the trees with beautiful leaves.
He watches over the little things I believe.
Leaves fall from branches, bleak and bare.
Dressed in all colors with nature's exquisite flair.

In all shapes, they fall in glittering winter wear.
The soft way they glide moves me to prayer.
Our God is a God of each little thing.
He causes the whispering wind to sing.

He guides each leaf softly to the earth,
Where it can help nature have a new birth.
He watches over them as they flutter and fall.
They dance as they leave the trees so tall.

He colors them like the rainbow.
No two are alike, with different shapes they flow.
We, like leaves, must fall and disappear.

Gently we fall with God's care so there's nothing to fear.

Like leaves our friend gave her life for others.

She helped so many, always doing for others.

Like a leaf, she must fall gently and softly to the earth.

Now, she too can live again and have a new birth.

I CAN SEE GOD

I can see God in my life each day.
Yes, I can see him in so many ways.
I can see him when I stop and look,
And read his Word from the Holy Book.

I see his carpet in the light blue sky,
Where all His beautiful birds do fly.
I see Him in nature's peaceful scene,
In the woodlands and meadows green.

And in his mountains rugged and strong,
I use my ears to hear nature's song.
He leads me where the flowers grow,
To see the violets and the wild rose.
He made the valleys and the streams,
He gave me beautiful youthful dreams.

With the sun, the clouds he can part,

If I believe he can open my heart.
He gives light to the moon and sun,
And turns on the stars when day is done.
God gives to earth snow and frost.
He makes the ocean waves to toss.

He gives to all cool fresh air.
All these things because He cares.
I hear him when church bells ring.
I can see him in all good things.
God keeps my heart aglow like fire,
This keeps me pressing on with desire.

I feel his love when I need it most,
I believe in God and the Holy Ghost.
I believe because this beauty I see.
God made this world for you and me.
He shows his beauty by the river-side.
He makes our path of life so wide.

His loveliness I see as I glance,

At colored leaves where sunbeams dance,

At magnificent jewel-like patterns on butterflies so rare,

And hear music from birds that fill the air.

Joyfully I travel his path at will,

Where I can hear soft music still.

I see him in the evening sun,

When the work of a happy day is done.

I BELIEVE IN ANGELS

In the realm of glory far beyond the blue,
God sends guardian angels to watch the things we do.

"See I am sending an angel before you, to guard you on the way and bring You to the place I have prepared" (Exodus 23:20).

"And suddenly there was a multitude of heavenly host With the Angel, praising God and saying: "Glory to God in the Highest and on earth peace to those on whom His favor rests" (Luke 2:13-14).

"And he sent out his angels with a trumpet blast and they will gather His elect from the four winds, from one end of the heavens to the other" (Matthew 24:31).

For Angels walk among us in ways we do not know,
To shelter us beneath wings and set our hearts aglow.

In daylight or in darkness, I have no need to fear.
I know that I'm protected by Angels hovering near.
Someday trumpets will sound from above.
What a glorious morning, I'll see God's eternal love.

*Have you ever gazed into the sky for a long time trying to see an angel? I did when I was very young. I never saw an angel in the sky, but I'm sure they exist.

There are highly intelligent and powerful spirts with distinct names and personalities. Some of them do us good while others want to harm us.

Angels are mentioned 400 times in the Bible. They are God's messengers, created long before the creation of man (Job 38:4-7).

THAT'S WHAT FAITH AND BELIEVING IS ALL ABOUT

Everything seems to happen so very slow.

Remember Jesus Christ had to grow.

Using thirty years to prepare for three,

He studied and worked, why shouldn't we?

He prepared himself by going to school.

In synagogues, he learned the Golden Rule.

He lived in a home caring for His Mother,

Supporting his younger sisters and brothers.

A carpenter, a craftsman, a builder by trade,

Doing honest hard work and not being afraid.

He was tempted by doubt and material things,

Invited to compromise and be a worldly king.

His mind whirling like lightning and thunder,

Baffled and enticed by sensation of wonder.

Even after His baptism more temptations came.

This will happen to us, just the same.

When we believe in him, our old life is gone.

We can make this change when we are all alone.

The worldly things are not the right way.

With love and faith, we can start a new day,

And stand ready to fight a good fight.

Sharing and loving and doing what's right.

He taught mercy and forgiveness from above,

Teaching, healing, and giving his great love.

Sharing with others while knowing he must die.

Sacrificing his life and knowing why.

He did this not to show that he was a man,

But to teach us to accept what we can't understand.

That's what faith and believing is all about.

From our tangled web, faith is the only way out.

With faith, our challenge becomes so clear,

Like Jesus we can face death without fear.

No longer a prisoner, torment will cease.

Free from the tangled web, we have true peace.

Yes! God is our answer, we can be sure,

With our life in God's hands, we are now secure.

MY MORNING IS NEAR

Darkness will fade with the morning,

A new day is dawning.

Early morn, a light, another day is here.

A new beginning, a challenge, I have no fear.

I thank the Lord for this day.

I ask God to help me on his way.

To forgive me for wasting yesterday.

To help me live the good life today,

And every tomorrow a dream of hope.

For one day at a time I can cope.

So, I look forward to this day,

As I let God lead the way.

As I travel life's road,

Lord help me carry the biggest load.

Secure in God's tender love,

Thankful for His blessing from above.

I'm filled with love, no more fear.

I know that my morning is near.

DARK IN THE VALLEY

The valley is full of sorrow and woe.

Yet, sorrow and troubles will help me to grow.

If life had no troubles and pain,

And without God's love I'd be living in vain.

The journey to the top is very slow.

Each day with God I must grow.

When the valley is dark I know what to do,

I trust the Lord to see me through.

He's the light along life's path,

Trust him, his love will always last.

When I feel pain, and think I'm lost,

I think of Christ on the cross.

Lord light my path, show me the way,

And use me to help others each day.

We all go through the dark valley.

This one thing I know, to reach the top
Through the dark valley, we must go.
On life's journey, I pray each day
That I can help someone find their way.

FIND PEACE

God is all-powerful, yet so kind.

He will lead us and hold our hand.

God will go with us all the way.

The wind and waves they obey.

We like the wind can be calm,

When Jesus holds us in His palm.

To the storm he said, "Be still."

We can be calm when we do His will.

When trouble seems to never cease,

Trust in Him. You will find peace.

HE

He made the universe a beautiful work of art.

He put his love within my heart.

Morning prayers make the day brighter.

Having faith makes my burdens lighter.

I enjoy simple things,

That each new morning brings.

With His spirit, I kneel and pray

That the world is in his care each day.

Love and inner-peace he can give,

And joy to our hearts wherever we live.

Life has so many precious things,

Like hearing a church bell ring.

On life's journey, they are all free.

God gives them to you and me.

In return we lend a helping hand,

As we travel through this beautiful land.

When our path is dark, we can't see without.

Following God's path is what life is all about.

On God's path, I can travel without fear,

Knowing that God is always near.

AN EASTER MORNING FEELING

There's no time like early morning that I feel quite so alive or so good. It's like being born into a new world with the cool clean morning air that seems to be filled with angels. As Matthew puts it, "The righteous shall shine forth as the sun in the kingdom of their Father."

I think that's the real promise of the morning. And the real reason why no matter what happens later in the day, each dawn gives a fresh opportunity to rise and shine.

Soon I come to my senses and the new world vanishes. I find myself as the same old person I was at bedtime.

There's a promise that the world will someday be born anew. We can wake up to the new life that God promised. All through the New Testament, every word within it turns around that most singular and consequential morning moment in all human history:

When Jesus awoke Easter morning, and the world really was born anew.

Awake my friend to the new life that God promised and give thanks to God for his blessings.

MY MORNING PRAYER

Never take a day for granted. Try to always smile. Cherish the little things. Remember to hug
The ones you really love. When good friends come to visit, it makes a bad day better.

When you grow old, it pays to have a sense of humor because you will do a lot of crazy and funny things that you don't mean to do. So, learn to laugh at yourself.

To be happy, you might need to have a bad memory of the past. Sometimes I have a good memory and sometimes I don't. But I always remember my morning prayer:

Father in Heaven I pray to you - my creator, friend, redeemer, savior. I pray to the Holy Spirit - my sustainer, comforter, counselor, and guide.

I come to you as a loving son, so thankful for all the blessings you have bestowed on my family. I come to you as a faithful servant, asking you to shape and mold me to be more like your Son, Jesus Christ.

Help me fulfill my purpose in life, using the gifts you have blessed me with. I pray with reverence to your holy name. I pray that your will be done and that I am in accordance with your will.

I pray for forgiveness of my sins, as I forgive others. I pray for strength and wisdom and courage to always do the right thing. Please, Lord, continue to nourish my family and me spiritually, emotional, and physically. Please stay on my mind, lips, and heart always.

I ask this all in the holy name of your Son, Jesus the Christ. Amen.

MY EVENING PRAYER

Dear Lord, forgive my sins.

Lord if I have caused one to go astray,

Forgive me, and teach me what to say.

Forgive me for trying to go my own way.

Lead me and guide me tomorrow, like today

Forgive my secret thoughts I do not see.

Father, help me live each day for thee.

And take me safely through this night,

Until I see the morning light.

PRAYER FOR TOMORROW

Lord, beyond today will be tomorrow.

Whether it will bring joy or sorrow,

I can only pray for your guidance.

Lord, each hour, each day,

Your strength to bare whatever may be

Your loving wisdom has for me.

So, sweet or bitter, sad or sweet or joy,

Be with me, Lord, beyond today.

BLESSING

For the hand that feeds us,

For the heart that loves us,

For the friends who comfort

And sustain us,

We thank thee, gracious Lord.

IF I COULD GIVE ADVICE TO YOUNG CHRISTIANS

If I could give advice to young Christians, this is what I'd say:

Faithful worship is essential to the growing Christian. Worship is where spiritual growth takes place. Discover what scripture says about spirituality and immerse yourself in it.

Shun spirituality that does not require commitment. Embrace friends in the faith wherever you find them. Eventually, return home and explore your own tradition. Never think you can advance by crushing others down. Don't worry about things that cannot be changed.

Don't fail to establish the habit of saving money. Check occasionally and make sure you haven't lost the things that money can't buy.

Goodness is the only investment that never fails.

Look for mature guides; honor wise leaders.

Don't travel life's journey without God as your guide.

Pray, and pray often.

WORRY

Why Worry? What can worry do?
It never keeps a trouble from overtaking you.
It gives you indigestion and sleepless hours at night.
And fills with gloom the days, however fair and bright.

It puts a frown upon the face, and sharpness to a tone
We're unfit to live with others and unfit to live alone.

Why worry? What can worry do?
It never keeps a trouble from overtaking you.

Why pray? What can praying do?
Praying really changes things, arranging life anew.
It's good for your digestion, gives peaceful sleep at night.
Fills the grayest, gloomiest day with rays of glowing light.

It puts a smile upon your face, the love note in your tone,
Makes you fit to live with others, and fit to live alone.

Why pray? What can praying do?

It brings God from heaven, to live and work with you.

IT'S ALMOST SPRING

I like what spring will bring,

Things like birds with speckled wings.

On the rooftop soft raindrops,

Me saying, "it's time to plant my vegetable crops.

In our yard the brown grass turns green.

And all the flowers bloom at once it seems.

The weather turns warm, I'm without a care.

I've shed my heavy underwear.

I start my garden, a work of art.

Planting marigolds is a big part.

I plant green beans with much care

Next to the squash growing there.

But they are not ready to pick yet,

Dogwoods must bloom, I must not forget.

Then it's time for fishing a little bit.

I'm ready, my fishing stuff is in my kit.

I know the fishing season is so brief,

Not to catch a few will bring me grief.

Alone with my rod and reel I depart,

Leaving my garden with a heavy heart.

It's the early morn as the sky turns blue,

And the cobwebs are sparkling with due,

With gnats and flies I am among,

And there's a snake darting out his tongue.

I hear the wind rustling the leaves,

I feel the morning's cool breeze.

Down at the pond I see fish so clear.

I forgot my bait, done this for years.

I use live worms, I have a few.

I have my rod and reel that is very new.

My luck, now raindrops start to fall,

Good for my crops, not good for fishing at all.

I get a bite, the cork twists and turns.

I jerk too hard; will I ever learn.

Now back to my garden all wet, I ride

Back at home with my hoe, I hit my stride.

For to have a garden the price is high.

I'm paying the price, I just give a sigh.

I plant my tomatoes and silver queen,

Soon my garden will be the best you've ever seen.

THE ABC'S OF SALVATION
ADMIT—BELIEVE—CONFESS

MY JOURNEY WITH THE MASTER

Everything from my past led me to this moment. I am now able to distinguish God's voice from the outer voices which fill my ears. He led me through each and every day of my life. Though so seldom did I recognize his leading. I thought that I was in charge, but I wasn't. Looking back, the mistakes are clear and how tenderly my Father in heaven dealt with them all.

Many a dangerous place he pulled me through. He knew I was not far enough along on my journey of faith to understand the things I did. My past holds many joys. These were accepted and their fullness appreciated, but even while I gave thanks daily for them in prayer, I saw him as someone far away too often.

Sorrow came into my life, like it does for us all. Now I am in a new era, I have come up and out of the valley of shadowy forms and misty thinking. My joys are the joys of the soul, and they are everlasting.

Now I am free in the knowledge which quickly returns to bless or curse me. So, I take heed of the little pitfalls like negative living, thinking, speaking, and writing. I keep my mind steadily on him each day, and as I go on my way I try to be a blessing to those who cross my path.

This journey has not been a short one for me. I did not step at once from my old self to a pure sense of believing and obeying. The journey is made up of little daily events, growth of love for the task ahead, and devotion to the people who are hurting and traveling the trail with me. I gladly help those who are ready to start this same journey.

With each step forward and upward with my maker, I have a feeling of freedom and joy that I cannot describe. The pathway will not always be smooth, for at times my senses will rebel, and days may pass in which they seem to have no meaning and no progress, I may at times seem to drop back again into the dark valley.

Today, I am still tested. But always I know that he is with me, that no matter what happens I can't be separated from Him.

I am on my journey to the mountaintop, and he will go with me all the way. As I travel with him, I find that things and people which pleased and satisfied me before, satisfy no longer. Things that made me happy do so no longer. Some old friends, whom I have left on another path, would find no more satisfaction in my company than I in theirs.

I am not lonely. He understands my hurts, my grief, and my human heart with all its desires and its longing for understanding. He is my companion always. He and the helper he has chosen to give me help along the way. I will also meet others, some will be ahead of me and they will reach back with willing hands to help me when the going gets tough. Others will take the place of the old pleasures as I go on my upward way. When I look back on the old path of attainment, I will feel like I am in another world, and I will now go forward clasping the hands of those who I now travel with.

I have learned that barriers across my path all have the same password: LOVE. I use this word freely and forcefully because with it comes joy.

God holds all things in the hollow of his hand. He unfolds life's deep meaning to me little by little so that with my understanding of him, I can let him work through me. My power is only the power he gives me.

REMEMBERING AND HISTORY

A FIREPLACE

For most of my life, I had the luxury of a wood burning fireplace. Today, I have gas logs. They do not offer the golden magic created in yesteryears by the old hearth.

I recall how the green oak wood sang a song as the blaze heated the sap making it boil and sizzle. Gazing into the red embers, I'd dream and let my imagination run wild in the winter. What a wonderful feeling it was to come in out of the snow to a friendly fireplace.

We'd roast sweet potatoes in the ashes or an apple on a string in front of the fire. On one side of the back porch we stacked wood for the fireplace and on the other side smaller pieces were stacked for the wood cook stove.

In the old days, we judged a farmer by the size of his woodpile. Dad made sure we had enough wood for the winter. He cut maple, oak and ash from behind our house. The woodpile was a big part of farm living before computers and moon shots.

In the mornings, the kitchen was the warmest place in the house. Now the wood stove is gone, just like the fireplace.

The good old days had their hardships and inconveniences. But viewed through the rosy glasses of my memory, they were romantic and fascinating. In those long-lost days of 'auld Lang sine' around the open fireplace, with the green wood singing, we could ask for no more.

A VISIT FROM GEORGE WASHINGTON BY THE YADKIN RIVER

In 1789, George Washington visited my Great, Great Grandfather, Michel Junger (Young) and his family for breakfast beside the Yadkin River.

Michael was my great, great, great grandfather, born in Germany.

The visit is noted in the Diary of George Washington, excerpt April 1791, Tuesday, 31

Left Salisbury about 4 o'clock; at 5 miles crossed the Yadkin the principal stream of the PeeDee and breakfasted on the north bank at Mr. Michael Young' place while my Carriages and horses were crossing. Fed my horses 10 miles farther, [Reeds, NC] at about 3 o'clock, after another halt, arrived at one of the Moravian towns 20 miles father – In all 35 miles from Salisbury. The road between Salisbury and Salem passes over very little sand but much that is different; being a good deal covered with Pine, but not sand. Salem a small but neat village; & like all the rest of the Moravian settlements, is governed by an excellent police – being within itself all kind of artisans – The number of souls does not exceed 200. [Washington was in Salem to meet Governor Martin that evening]

Before Washington arrived, a horseback rider notified Michel that Washington would be there for breakfast the next morning. Michel notified his son, Barney, who lived up the road. The wives made a country ham breakfast.

The men ate inside the house while the children watched Washington's men feed their horses. One of the boys got to climb onto George Washington's buggy.

THE BEST YEARS OF MY LIFE

Growing up in the Yadkin Mill Village, just above the Yadkin river, in the early 1900s I had ample time to smell, taste, and touch God's magnificent handiwork. Being outside most of the summer was a sure way to experience God's wonders.

In this small tight-knit community, we all felt like one big family. I walked everywhere - school, corner store, my cousin's house, my big rock, river, old toll bridge, baseball field, Boy Scout cabin, church.

I most enjoyed walking to church on Sunday morning and ringing the church bell. Each time I opened the front door of that little red brick church on a hill, I thought I saw Jesus inside. I worshiped much of my life in the beauty of that little church.

Each morning during the week, I'd deliver newspapers all over the village. Then I'd go to the church where the door was always unlocked and take up my job to keep the church clean. In winter, I'd build a fire in church's stoves and ring the bell every Sunday morning.

That little red brick church on a hill inspired me to live a Christian life because there I was taught that God is good all the time.

My memory tells me that the best years of my life were when I was young and living in the Yadkin Mill Village. But that is not really true. Nothing is more rewarding than my great grandparent years.

It's here as a great grandparent that I've learned wisdom and true love. It's this part of life that if I use my time wisely, God might use me to shape the next generation.

"And the peace of God, which transcends all understanding, will guard your hearts and your minds in Christ Jesus." -Philippians 4:7

WINTER ON THE POND

The pond was a meeting place winter and summer back in "the good old days." It was really a creek, called Shupin's creek, with a wide mouth flowing in the Yadkin River.

One winter day when school was out and the ground was covered with 12 inches of snow, I headed out early for the pond. The air was still cracking cold. When I got to the pond, I saw a red-tailed hawk, the only one I have ever seen. It circled the pond as if looking for something, maybe food. I knew he must have been hungry. I saw his yellow long legs and his yellow eyes just searching over the ice. He turned and seemed to float over to a dead tree and landed near two wood-peckers just pecking away at a hole and pulling out sleeping Grubb worms.

I followed rabbit tracks almost to the pond's edge. But just before I got there, I saw fox tracks cross the rabbit tracks. I wondered if the fox caught the rabbit or not. Then I spotted rabbit. He was looking up at the woodpeckers. I crept closer to rabbit. When he saw me, rabbit jumped up high and landed on iced over pond. I chuckled as he slid half way across the pond on his belly.

Soon I got to work pushing snow back to make way for a small circle. With a few pieces of dead wood, the fire soon crackled. I got to thinking about all the fish and turtles and frogs that were so plentiful in the summer, but now they were under the ice. Maybe the turtles and frogs were asleep in the mud. And where were the snakes, I guessed they were in holes in the ground under all the snow. I was thought, how do they make it until summer? I guess all the insects are asleep. I wondered how they survived the winter with all the snow and ice.

That's the secret of Mother Nature, she takes care of sleeping creatures under the snow, icy pond, and mud.

Soon many of my friends showed up, and I stopped daydreaming and watching the creatures to build the fire up bigger and to play "Tag" on the ice in our old-fashioned skates.

MEMORIES OF MY YOUTH

Good memories come to me in the night,
Long before the morning light.
As my golden years start to unfold,
I just don't have to grow old.
I can't go back and change the past.
Only love and good memories can last.

Memories of seesaws and grapevine swings,
Playing made-up games and making my playthings.
Playing Old Maid, checkers and jacks,
Three-legged races and racing in a sack.
Digging a cave in the side of a hill,
Riding in a buggy, what a thrill.

Feeding hobos who knocked on our door,
Buying ice cream at Martin's store.
Saving my chewing gum on a bedpost,

Cooking over a fire at a wiener-roast.

Visiting my grandfather on his farm,

Climbing a hayloft ladder in his barn.

Tying two cans together with a string,

Making a phone, what a fun thing.

A gourd dipper, a spring, a cool drink,

Catching lighting-bugs, watching them blink.

Under a big tent, a traveling picture show.

Everyone in Yadkin was sure to go.

When the villain grabbed Pearl White,

Then, To Be Continued next Saturday night.

We watched a flood from the old toll bridge.

We gathered nuts from Chestnut Ridge.

On the railroad bridge, we climbed over the edge.

Then a freight train roared over our heads.

It was supper time, time to head back.

We returned home following the railroad tracks.
Memories of the honor of being a Boy Scout,
Having fun with the troop camping out.

Playing every kind of game with a ball.
Climbing the high rocks afraid I'd fall.

Family fun brings memories galore.
Memories of the checked apron Mama wore.
She wore it to do all her many chores.
She wore it to do her work out-of-doors.

She sometimes used it to wipe my nose.
And to hold clothespins to hang up clothes.
There was never a day she didn't have it on.
How I miss that apron now that she is gone.
Each Sunday the church bell I'd ring,
Calling the people to worship.

Aunt Alice played on the old organ keys,

And Dad would pray down on his knees.

We kids behaved until the sermon was done.

Then to the river we would run.

Now those years have long gone,

I'm beholden to Yadkin, I call home.

There's no end to the memories I hold.

With good memories, I'll never grow old.

FLOUR SACK UNDERWEAR

When I was just a little lad,

My Mama made my underwear.

With seven kids and Pa's poor pay,

Things made with flour sacks was the way.

Flour sacks for quilts stood the test.

Sometimes a Gold Medal Seal was on my chest.

My shirts and britches, she made them all.

On my pants, a Self-Rising sign, I recall.

Sometimes an advertisement was on my back,

Because we never wasted a flour sack.

Some were Gold Medal and some were Pillsbury's, too.

They were stamped purple and blue.

We emptied the sack and then swept.

The string on top was always kept

We filled sacks with feathers and down,

Made pillows and our sleeping gowns.

A flour sack was my school book bag.

One was used under the saddle of our nag.

They were bleached and sewn and worn.

As diapers, bibs, and shirts that we adorned.

Mama made skirts, blouses and slips.

She made rugs from flour sack strips.

She made curtains for our old shack,

From the humble flour sack.

Used for a sling when a bone would break,

And Mama even used one to wrap up a molasses cake.

They were hung on the wall to cover cracks.

They were sturdy albeit common, our flour sacks.

Flour sacks were tough, they'd never tear.

Every clothesline hung with sack underwear.

Everyone wore them, we had nothing to hide.

THE FAMILY POT

As far back in childhood as my memory can go,
A household vessel greets me that wasn't meant to show.
Beneath a bed 'twas' anchored, where only few could see,
A large ceramic crock, for use in privacy.

Some called the critter a jar, some called it thunder mug.
Others called it badger and a few called it the jug.

To bring it in at evening was bad enough no doubt.
But heaven help the person who had to take it out.

When nights were dark and stormy, it was a useful urn.
On icy winter mornings, the rim it seemed to burn.
Today's modern facility relieves me of a lot,
And only in my memory do I see the family pot.

HOMEMADE GAMES

We made up games and had much fun,

Using sticks for swords and guns.

We made our own toys and kites,

We shared and seldom had fights.

King of the mountain was rough,

Our games taught us to be tough.

We'd fight to see who could be king.

We could shoot marbles out of a ring.

We played hopscotch most every day,

To be with the girls, this was the way.

Girls were good at jumping rope,

To jump as good as them was our hope.

We played baseball and didn't keep score.

Why don't children play jacks anymore?

We made tom-walkers and walked on cans.

We made slingshots from rubber bands,

And played punch-back and hide-and-seek.

Our swimming pool was at the creek.

We turned somersaults and played many games.

Now kids only watch TV, what a shame.

We had grapevine swings to carry us away.

If I could turn back time, I'd swing all day.

I'd stop only for some homemade ice cream,

And think about the games we played,

And the picnics, hot dogs and lemonade,

And dream of the homemade games we played.

THE MAGIC AND MYSTERY OF YOUTH

Remembering the joy of the out-of-doors,
Where meadows use flowers for a floor.
Seeing rolling fields ready for harvest.
Breathing in the odor of the forest.
Seeing shining webs in the morning dew.

All this beauty only seen by a few.
Watching the early sky turn blue,
With clouds opening like a curtain.
A doorway to Heaven, I'm certain.

Cool wind whispering in the trees,
In the shade of a tree feeling free.
At the river seeing the water below,
In my green canoe, away I'd go.

Resting under a willow in the shade.

Fishing with a pole, it's the only way.

To feel a loose line tighten, another fish caught.

So many memories fishing have brought.

Camping and sleeping in the rain.

A bed on roots and rocks causing pain.

Hearing an owl at midnight.

Seeing a formation of geese in flight.

I've learned much from the out-of-doors,

Learned where squirrel's pecans are stored.

Learned where birds build their nest,

High or low they know which is best.

Know where the rabbit makes his bed.

I've watched little birds being fed.

Learned the secrets of the creatures.

Know their ways and all their features.

Learned many outdoor arts and crafts.

Made kites, slingshots, built a raft.

Shot copperheads while canoe drifting.

Kept a King snake for a pet.

Fed baby squirrels from my hand.

Found a clear pond almost hidden,

Where bathing suits were forbidden.

One thing I enjoyed the best

Was the splendor of a colored sunset.

Soon out of childhood into manhood,

Still in my canoe, taking chances.

Hearing birds singing in tree branches,

Learning from Mother Nature many truths.

Remembering the magic and mystery of youth.

THE OLD SMOKEHOUSE

The meat that once hung in the old smokehouse
Was killed and cured by the woman's spouse.
He would make a garden, and she would can.
Lots of food was prepared by the woman's hand.

Our grandparents knew just how things were done,
But the art was lost to their daughters and sons.
Why should dogs teach their pups to hunt,
When store-bought food leaves no want.
Cats don't teach kittens to search for prey,
There's food in their dish every day.

How would we survive without the store?
We don't have a garden,
Nor a smokehouse anymore.

MY BANTAM ROOSTER

I had a rooster once, I want you to know

And I loved to hear him crow.

Our old rooster was getting awful lazy,

But not my Bantam rooster I got from Stacy.

He was the cock of the walk too,

He was small, never seemed to grow.

Feathers black and head erect,

From the hens, he had respect.

He would strut if it were cold or hot.

To the hens, he was Johnny-on-the-spot.

He'd peck the big rooster on the throat.

He was a fighter of some note.

To be in charge was his way,

As he would strut around all day.

The hens would scratch him his worms.

Everything was done on his terms.

Until he crossed our dog, Grover.

Then, my Bantam rooster's days were over.

REMINISCING AS I GROW OLDER

It seems like just a short time ago,
With peace of mind I started to grow.
I could hear music and church bells ringing.
I marveled at the blue skies and birds singing.

Many memories of lemonade, rainbows, and games.
A kind of happiness that's hard to explain.
Cracking walnuts in the shade of a tree,
Feeling a cool breeze and feeling free.

A bag of marbles and a kite of broom sedge,
Catching butterflies, keeping a rabbit in a cage.
Spinning tops, playing so many fun games.
Every new day full of joy and never the same.

A spring, a gourd dipper, tadpoles, how enchanted,
Beautiful flowers growing but were not planted.

Just living with beautiful roses and fresh air,

And knowing that with love God put them there.

MY LAST TRIP TO THE OLD HOME PLACE

Today, I took my last trip to the Yadkin River,
My old home place. It's now called High Rock Lake.

Way back when, it was the Yadkin River, flowing free.
It's not the same place I remember it to be.
It's not the happy place I grew up long ago.
It's now an ugly place, it has changed so.

In my day, it was a beautiful place to be around.
A place where happiness could be found,
Where all of nature's beauty I could see.
It's not there anymore, how can this be?

Gone is the place I tied my canoe to a dock,
And where I hid my treasures in the rocks.
Through memory's door, I see a big oak tree,
The one I used to climb to feel the breeze,

A grapevine swing across a stream,

Green grass to lie upon and dream.

I'd climb 'the old possum hollow tree,'

With not a worry in the world, feeling free.

I'd run into the wide-open fields, as if an open door,

It's strange, it's not like that anymore.

I look in vain for the big mulberry trees,

Remembering when I played marbles on my knees.

Fields are gone where watermelons used to grow.

It's not the same old home place, I used to know.

In memories, I treasure this place with joy.

I thank God for the home place I knew as a boy.

BLACKEYED PEA BLUES

I once hoped another black-eyed pea to see.
I've picked bushels since I was young,
Beneath the hot Carolina sun.

We'd take our buckets or sacks or whatever,
And set out on a mission, the pea patch to gather.
Up one row and down the other,
It mattered not what else we'd ruther.

Mama'd say, "Get busy before it gets too hot,"
Then she'd look to see how many peas we'd got.
Entangled among the pea vines, we'd hope
To find a watermelon or a cantaloupe.

The gathering sometimes could be quite fun,
But the dreaded shelling still had to be done.
Whenever we'd gathered a bushel or three,
You'd find us on a screened-in porch or under a tree.

With a tub for the hulls and peas in our laps,

We'd make conversation, and string, shell and snap.

Our eyes became blurred our fingers got numb,

But we knew to keep at it, if we were ever to get done.

We'd sit and shell, and shell and sit,

And we welcomed any help that we could get.

Any cousin, neighbor or friend soon

Walked into a trap, if they wondered in.

A mess of full jars on the cellar shelves,

Made us feel so rewarded and proud of ourselves.

Knowing our family would have them to eat,

When the cold winter came with the snow and sleet.

They would taste so good, with the smokehouse hams,

Some cornbread, onions and candied yams.

I'm really just having a little rhyming fun,

I love black-eyed peas, when all's said and done!

THE OPEN FIREPLACE

Like the front porch that's almost gone,
The old fireplace is fast moving on.
Lost in many homes, a thing of the past,
Like so many good things that didn't last.

We shared togetherness by our fireplace,
With its flames of bright scarlet lace.
It makes me sad to think of its passing.
To me it had a spirit that was everlasting.
By the fire sharing joy and love with each other,
Here my family listened close to our mother.

Dad at the fireplace with pipe and the Good Book,
Me nodding and dreaming in a warm nook.
Falling asleep with a wood fire burning,
Me with happy memories and pleasant yearning.

Roasting apples on a string, popcorn popping,

Parching peanuts and little sparks hopping.

Sweet potatoes roasting in ashes and coals,

Pot of beans cooking, eating all I could hold.

For bad colds, we sometimes roasted onions,

While Granddad sat trimming his bunions.

Roasted marshmallows while the fire burnt low,

Giving off the colors of a rainbow.

Children coming in with half-frozen toes,

By the fireplace, socks hanging in a row.

While we warmed blankets to take to bed,

Now our prayers and good thoughts in our heads.

Back of the house, a big woodpile in a stack.

Above the fireplace, books on a rack.

Our fireplace shining through the mist of years,

In my memory, that open fireplace always appears.

Warming us inside and out, it can't be beat.

When friends drop in, it was the place to meet,

For storytelling time as the fire burned low.

How can families let the open fireplace go?

By our open fireplace our lives were good.

I'd never change all this, even if I could.

A FRONT PORCH

Houses aren't built with porches any more.
No porch swing, no welcome mat at the door.
Houses everywhere, yet no porches do I see.
New ones without a porch, how can that be?

The age of the front porch has passed us by.
I look back on porch memories with a sigh.
I know a front porch is what we need.
A porch with a rocker and a book to read.

We have lost a place for friends and fun,
Lost a place where we can meet new ones.
A place where neighbors can meet is gone.
Gone like so many good things. What's wrong?

There's no place like a porch, I'd say,
For grown-ups to watch their children play.
Growing up, a porch is the best place to be.

Our front porch made joyful memories for me.

The old porch swing gave joy and fun,
Here I could sleep in the evening sun.
The squeaking chain saying, "All is well."
If it could talk what stories it would tell.

A front porch was where people could talk,
Friends could drop in after an evening walk.
A place for entertainment, sometimes a song,
Always storytelling, but now the porch is gone.

We shared our porch with a family of wrens,
We shared it with our neighbors and friends.
They taught us the art of storytelling, of course.
We learned this lost art from our front porch.

Our porch was filled with happy sounds back then,
And stories of places where I'd never been.
Neighbors would tell ghost stories year after year,

This closeness and fun time is gone, I fear.

Dad would tell of the past and good times.
They were stories without profanity, violence, or crime.
These yarns would leave good thoughts to stir us deep,
Then with pleasant dreams we'd fall asleep.

Here the sharing of stories produced a form of wealth.
We had no problems with mental health.
With a front porch, there's no need to roam.
All our problems can be solved at home.
People could have porches if they would,
And I would bring porches back if I could.

WATERMELON

I could never eat watermelon at a table.

To eat with a knife and spoon I was never able.

In a restaurant is not the place.

Watermelon in little balls, what a waste.

Sitting up straight is not the way.

There's two places on a hot day,

To eat watermelon, I'd say.

One is the backyard cause here there's no need,

For a napkin or worry about the seed.

The chickens will pick them up, have no fears.

Well, all, except the ones in your ears.

Here the slices can be very big,

You can throw the rinds to the pig.

But the best place of all is in the patch,

Where you have a choice from the whole batch.

You thump until you hear the dead-ripe thump.

Then bust it open, and sit on your rump.

Here in the patch you can eat and eat.

That's watermelon eating that can't be beat.

CASTOR OIL

Old-fashion remedies are not for me,

Like Sulphur and molasses and sassafras tea,

Cherry bark, Epson salts. and castor oil.

Don't even like fatback meat on a festered boil.

Wearing a sack of asafetida around my neck,

Even the odor could make you a wreck.

I licked the bitter stuff from a spoon,

And thought that spring came to soon.

For these remedies were given in the spring.

They thought good health they would bring.

How could castor oil produce a robust race,

For in my case, it was much too late.

For castor oil, I had the most hate.

That's one remedy, I'll never take.

While very young I made a vow,

That castor oil would never touch my bowel.

I dreamed of no castor oil for the next generation,

I hoped it would be outlawed in our nation.

Just give me liberty or death as I toil,

But never, never give me castor oil.

COUNTRY CHURCHES AND COUNTRY PREACHERS

Way back when, we attended Smith Grove Baptist church out in the country. In my later years, we faithfully attended the friendly church with a pipe organ just down the street - The First Baptist Church of Lexington.

In my earlier years, churches, like Smith Grove, consisted of one big room with a wood stove for heat and a box around the stove full of sand. I think the sand was for the tobacco spit. On the right-hand side of the preacher, stood four rows of short benches for the choir. In front of the choir was an organ, which my granddaddy Young played when the regular lady was absent. Little shelves built into the wall held kerosene lamps.

The preachers back then had very little book learning like they do today. But they knew the Bible, and I believe the Lord was with them just the same. Cause after all, didn't God love Simon Peter just as much as he did Paul?

The preachers back then preached hell-fire and brimstone. The preachers I remember seemed old to me, with white hair, and some with long white beards. Once I asked Mother, "Is that God?"

She smiled and said, "No, you can't see God. That's only the preacher."

I believe that the old preachers could comfort a body when one was troubled or disheartened. I remember Dad saying that when Brother Theo preached you could hear a pin drop. But Dad didn't like him so much because he preached about women a-wearing powder and paint, smoking, and he called them modern Jezebels.

I guess Preacher Carrack was Mom and Dad's favorite one. He sometimes ate Sunday dinner with us. And I felt good being around him. Dad said preacher Carrack had a good voice, and it looked like he was winding his sermon up to fling it out to the congregation each Sunday morning.

Back then the preachers didn't stand in one place and preach in a quiet voice. There was no danger of any one going to sleep. Sometimes the preacher would come down the aisle among the congregation. I remember once being scared to death as he came close to me and Mother. He looked me right in the eyes.

Once this same preacher preached his whole sermon behind the lectern. His wife later told my Mother that his pants had come open in front. She said at the closing prayer, when all heads were bowed, he remedied the situation.

Times have changed, but I hold on to memories and remember the dear preachers who visited me when I was sick, just like our preacher does now. Back then the preacher got down on his knees to pray when he came to visit us when we were sick. Now we hold hands while the preacher prays, and what a blessing it is to hear our preacher pray.

DAD AND HIS MULE

Over and around the hill trailed dad behind a mule pulling a plow.

Said my dad to the mule, "Mack, you're the son of a jackass and I am a man made in the image of God. Yet here we are hitched together year in and year out. I often wonder if you work for me or I work for you.

Sometimes I think this is a partnership between a mule and a fool. For surely, I work just as hard as you do if not harder. When plowing we cover the same distance, but you do it on four legs and I do it on two. Mathematically speaking I do twice as much work as you.

Soon we'll be preparing for another crop of corn. When it is harvested, one third goes to pay for the fertilizer. Another third goes to you and what little there is left is mine. But, you eat your third, and I have to divide my share with the banker, my family of nine, and the chickens and ducks.

Old Mack, you're getting the best of me. It just ain't fair for a mule, the son of a jackass, to rob a man who is created in the image of God. And come to think about it, you only help cultivate the ground. Then I have to cut, harvest, shuck, and shell the corn while you look over the fence and 'hee-haw' at me.

All of the fall months and part of the winter, the whole family picks the cotton to make some money to pay the interest on the mortgage, pay the taxes on the land, and to buy harness for you! But none of this worries you. No, not one bit. You just leave that to me, you ungrateful ornery cuss.

About the only time I get the long end of the rope is on election day. I can vote and you can't. So, I'm wondering who is the jackass after all, me or you.

DOWN MEMORY LANE

The Yadkin River is where I'll begin,
With my buddies, we'd all jump in.
Walking alone on riverbanks seemed so long.
Trying to hum a church song.

I'm happy to go down memory lane,
With no worries about loss or gain.
I'm free to watch the river flow,
And smell the flowers as they grow.

This closed in feeling is long gone,
As I whistle a happy tune.
With memories of a lone whippoorwill,
And a full moon over Mill Village Hill.

This is what happiness is all about,
With memories of a two-room school house.
Where we learned our lessons very well,

I still hear the teacher ringing the bell.

Four grades in one room side by side,

We learned from each other with much pride.

We learned book learning and much more,

Childhood memories has opened another door.

FOR THE LOVE OF CHITTERLING

When cold weather sets in, its hog killing time in my mind. I looked forward to hog killing day. It was a special occasion for the whole community, working hard together to prepare our sustenance, and enjoying the fellowship. Hard cider was frequently tapped.

Hog killing was truly a community event in Yadkin. Everyone had one or two hogs. My Dad was a specialist in hog killing. He'd place the barrel of his 22 pistol squarely between the hog's eyes. Then real- quick with a sharp butcher knife, he'd skillfully split the hog's throat from side to side with one swift motion.

A hardwood fire blazed to boil a big pot of water. The hog would be immersed several times for scalding.

Then came the hard part - picking the hair off the hog by hand. From there, the hog was hung on a pole between two larger poles firmly planted in the ground and scraped real-good. A gangling stick two or three feet long was inserted through the tendons in the hind feet for removing the inside "stuff" with a sharp knife. The smell, oh how strong.

Tubs stood ready for separating the parts. Mr. Simmerson took the hair to fertilize his next year's crop of corn. I can still see the white bodies of the hogs slit from neck to tail hanging on a cross-bar.

The large intestines were emptied, cleaned and soaked for seven days to make chittlings. What a nourishing dish so overlooked or ignored today. The Yankees have never been able to savor the delicately browned pieces of gustatorial delight which we Southerners swear by.

Chitterling must be akin to Manna in vitamin contents. It's oh so tasty too. My daddy sometimes ate a little before the frying by dashing a little vinegar on the hot chitterlings. That first thorough cleaning is awfully important. Chitterlings have a very unpleasant odor while parboiling, and some cooks compare it with collard greens cooking. A big slug of whiskey is said to be conductive to digestion while eating chitterlings.

The small intestines were slit to remove their contents, washed, and hung to dry for soap making. Some of the intestines were carefully selected and prepared for sausage stuffing too.

The head and feet were given to the women for special treatment. The jaws we packed in salt and cooked on New Year's Day with black-eyed peas. The brains we ate with scrambled eggs for breakfast. The livers got cooked and ground for liver pudding. Ears, snouts and feet were boiled in water until done. All the meat was removed from the bones and cut into small pieces. Us youngsters sometimes helped with this.

Those pieces of meat returned to the meat stock and were set aside to jell for making the savoriest dish of all called "SOUCEMEAT." We sometimes kept a few feet for pickling in a large crock. I had no use for them, but boy did my dad love that treat.

As a kid, I sought the hog bladder to dry out and blow up so we could knock it around like a volleyball. Some were made into rattles by adding shot or 'pee-dabs' (marbles). Sometimes I'd pop one by jumping up and down on it to hear the noise like an exploding firecracker.

Then on the second day, we cut and salted down hams, shoulders, spareribs, and side meat after cutting off the fat for lard and soap and "Cracklings" that made the best darn cornbread.

FAMILY MEMORIES

I have so many memories stored away,
Just saving up for a lonely day.
A small home by a fire, a warm spot.
Roses blooming and a garden plot,
Cedar trees and shade trees galore,
Dogwood tree blooming outside the front door.

Back yard maples where I'd rest my eyes,
Green garden, sunshine, and open skies,
Then within me, my thoughts inspired,
With the family standing around a fire.

Grown-ups and children united all,
Sticking together, whatever befalls.
Laughing a lot in happy release,
A household blessed with much peace.
Memories for me to store away,
Hopefully will bring joy on another day.

YADKIN RIVER INDIANS

Today I think of the forgotten men,

On Yadkin hill their lives came to an end.

I remember Indian graves where they lay dead.

Down in the bottomland where deer used to graze,

I hear cries of the Red Man echoing through the age.

My love for the Indians I cannot describe,

But I know on this same trail walked the Sapona tribe.

A One-Eyed Chief made this land his home.

On this river trail his brave warriors roamed.

If only the pottery and arrows could talk,

And tell me their history while I walk.

Many moons have passed since they departed this place.

But I still see many a beautiful Indian trace.

Here is where birchbark canoes once cruised.

I find many relics left where they were last used.

In my dreams, I bring them back to this rich soil
When they were without war or toil.

Here is where a Wigwam made his home.
Right here in these woods where Boy Scouts now roam.
Here the Yadkin Indians can only live again in spirit.
His war dance, his campfire, in dreams I see it.
I see Indian boys on the river catching fish.
I look across the mighty Yadkin and make a wish.
It is to call him Brother and claim a little kin
To the Indians, who treaded the banks on the Yadkin.

Now only the wise old owl guards this sacred soil
Where once brave warriors did hunt and fight and toil.
I walk through his hunting ground with a heavy heart.
We drove him from his land, still he left his mark.

All is now passed away; his arrows are broken.
Here and there a few pieces, my only token.
No longer can his echoing war whoops be heard.

Slowly, sadly I climb another hill without a word.

He was friendly at first, giving his trust.
We gave him disease, false promises till he'd had enough.
Warriors fought to settle the score.
But outnumbered, his war cry is heard no more.
Only a hurt whisper could be heard,
As he left Yadkin, his home without a word.
We broke his heart, tried to break his will,
His memory and history we cannot kill.

From his happy hunting ground to his grave he creeps.
Silently on this Yadkin hill, I kneel and weep.

WOODSTOVE COOKING

My mother cooked delicious pies and cakes, fried chicken, beef-roast, fluffy rice, and the best pinto beans and big hot biscuits you can imagine on an old woodstove, with no temperature controls for the oven. She controlled the heat by the fire in the firebox.

As the cook in our family, I still fix old-timey down-home meals. The kind of supper with fresh black-eyed peas that took hours to shell, stewed corn that flew up to the kitchen window when scraped off the cob, red, marble-sized Irish potatoes from the garden peeled and boiled just so and slathered in butter.

I fix a lot of greens and pies and cakes and persimmon pudding. There's lots of everything leftover for freezing and eaten later. Next week I'll stand in front of the old upright freezer and say, "Now what left-overs will we have for supper?"

With the left over left-overs I add lots of onions and call it Goulash. When we get tired of that at suppertime, I fix scrambled eggs, grits, liver mush, and hot biscuits. They all say, "Daddy, that's the best supper yet."

PERSIMMONS

Have you ever bit into a green persimmon? It's been a long time, but I still remember the effects of a not so ripe persimmon. If you want your jaws to lock, your eyes to bulge, tears to run down your cheeks, your hair to stand on end, and to endure a real physical shock, take a bite of a green persimmon. Opossums and raccoons feast on ripe persimmons but not green ones.

On our farm stood two large persimmon trees. We ate a lot of persimmon pudding, highly seasoned with spices. My dad built a fence around the persimmon tree and put his pigs inside so they would eat those ripe persimmons and keep us from tracking them in the house.

Persimmon wood is good for many a thing like golf clubs, loom shuttles, and firewood. There's nothing better than a forked persimmon branch in the hands of the right person for divining deep veins of fresh water.

Some among us made persimmon beer; it's not intoxicating. The recipe is simple: five pounds of persimmons, one and one half pound of sugar, one gallon of water, two crushed Campden tablets, two packs of all-purpose wine yeast, and a pack of nutrients.

WHEN PAPA SHAVED

Every Saturday afternoon and Wednesday night,
Papa got his shaving things and set them up just right.
"Ruby, bring the looking glass," he never failed to call.
"The one above the comb case hanging in the hall."
Maggie, put the kettle on; Jimmy, chop some wood;
Guy, you and Martin bring it in and fill the box up good.
Willie, draw some water; Mama, where's my strop?"
Oh, everybody had his job, and each one had to hop.

Then he'd pluck a hair and hold it in the light,
Testing the razor's sharpness to see that it was just right.
And then he'd strop a little more, and pluck another hair,
Till along the razor's edge the cut was clean and square.
He'd pull his face from side to side to tighten up the skin,
First of the cheek, then throat, lips, and chin.
"Someday you boys will know what trouble it will be
To do this once or twice a week, just wait and see."

But my children never knew that I shaved every day.
Within my tiny bathroom, they'd just be in the way.
Now children care still less about their daddy's needs.
They are busy with their own many deeds.

Sometimes I get lonesome, and wish we could have saved
The family solidarity we had when Papa shaved.

WHEN MOTHER MADE AN ANGEL CAKE

When mother baked an angel cake, kids gather'd round

To watch her hands at work yet never make a sound.

We'd watch her stir the eggs and powdered sugar too.

She'd pour it in a crinkled tin, then when it was through,

She spread the icing over it, and we knew very soon

We'd get the plate to lick and one would get the spoon.

No matter where we were those mornings at play,

Upstairs or out of doors, we all knew right away.

Ma was in the kitchen getting out the tins

To make an angel cake, and so we scampered in.

She would smile at us and say, "Now you keep still till I tell you when."

She'd kneel by the stove, and put her arm inside so white,

To find if it was heating up ust right.

Mouths and eyes open because we always knew

The time for us to get our taste was quickly coming due.

While mixing the icing up, she hummed a simple tune.
One would lick the plate and one would lick the spoon.
If we could glimpse heaven and some kitchen there,
I'm sure we'd see mother smiling and still just as fair.

I know that gathered round her stands an angel brood.
They too are watching as she makes her angel food.
I know that little angels, like us, are never late.
At any moment, she'll let them lick spoon and plate.

CORDUROY WHISTLE BRITCHES

While I was going to school at Yadkin's two-room schoolhouse, I wore corduroy britches. We called them "Whistle britches" they were sturdy ribbed cloth made from cotton (in those days); they were durable and suitable for britches.

The britches would whistle when I walked up to sharpen my pencil. I created a whistling sound when my knees rubbed together in the quite schoolroom. Everyone laughed. It was quite embarrassing, and it was more so when I walked in and out of the church.

But sometimes it was fun making my britches whistle.

CORN SHUCKINGS

a corn shucking really meant neighbors helping neighbors. All the folks in the community would gather together and assist each other shuck their corn. When the crop was large, the farmer would have his corn dumped in a long pile in the barnyard. Folks would come for dinner and shuck the corn in the afternoon. After which, there would be a delicious supper served by the women folk.

With two pots full of chicken and dumplings and another pot of roast beef and jellies, preserves, butter, biscuits as large as your fist, and vegetables of all kind, it was a cornucopia.

The pie shucking is where the folks came after supper and shucked the corn by lantern light. Then they'd go in the house and eat pies of all kind by the hundreds. The men shucking the corn talked and joked and laughed.

The ones that liked corn liquor hid a bottle in the corn pile, but never drank too much.

The men folk went in to eat first, then the children. The women folks were the last to eat about nine o'clock. While they were eating, the men built a fire in the barn yard and the star performers got their fiddles and banjos out and got going with, "Turkey In The Straw," "Swing Your Partner", and "She'll be coming around the Mountain When She Comes," The young folks paired off on the porch to have a candy pulling. The evening of fun continued until midnight and many much later.

Us kids played games like 'hide and go seek'. Some of the kids even played 'spin-the-bottle. When one of us boys shucked a red ear of corn, we got to try and kiss the girl of our choice. The one with the red ear of corn would throw it at the girl, and then he had to catch her.

Back in those days most girls got their first kiss at a corn shucking. Sometimes the girl would pick up the red ear of corn and keep it as a 'keep-sake.' Other girls would throw the red ear back at the boy and run away. A lot of young people became sweethearts at corn shuckings.

Money was scarce back then, but we had plenty of muscle. I think there was a spirit of helpfulness that is not present these days. Even though a few men made frequent trips behind the barn for a snort of mountain dew just to pep up their appetites, all in all, a corn shucking was quite a big thing, a helpful, friendly event always enjoyed by all us down to earth dirt farmers.

IF I COULD GO BACK TO THE LITTLE HOUSE WHERE I SPENT MY FIRST 25 YEARS WITH MOM AND DAD

If I could go back, I would look Mom and Dad straight in their eyes, and here's what I would say:

"I love you. I appreciate the way you raised me. You taught me right from wrong and what character ought to be. You taught me that everyone is important.

Mom, you taught me to not say anything bad about anyone. You taught me responsibility and honesty, which I have tried to follow in my life. You also taught me to love tiny wild flowers.

Thinking back, you taught me that there is a God and that he is good all the time. And that he loves me, and how important faith is in life.

Dad, you taught me sportsmanship and to be kind to everyone and to laugh often. You taught me how to survive and to enjoy this beautiful country we live in and to have a little fun and play baseball."

If there was still time, when I went back, I would like to go with Dad to feed the chickens and hogs, then down to the river and look his fish baskets. I'd eat Mom's good supper with her hot biscuits.

Afterwards we'd sit on the front porch and talk and laugh. I would pick a red rose from Mom's rose bush and give it to her with a kiss and tell her again that I love her. I'd tell them both again that I love them, and I'd give them a big hug.

Then back in the present, I'd give thanks to God for giving me so many years with Mom and Dad and for the knowledge that they are at peace forever. It's that knowing that makes the joy outweigh the sorrow of having had to say good-bye to them.

MAKING MOLASSES

I can't remember a time when we didn't have molasses in a barrel in our smokehouse with a ham and shoulder hanging nearby.

When I was about five, my dad took me along to the molasses mill where Mr. Beck made the best molasses anywhere to be found. He hitched up old Maud, our horse, to the wagon loaded down with sugar cane. I sat on top of the sugar cane. Dad said to be careful because the cane would cut me if I moved around too much.

At the mill, two large steel rollers mounted on wooden blocks with a long shaft extended several yards out. A horse was harnessed to that contraption. He walked in a circle, turning the rollers, which crushed the cane stalks that were fed between the rollers by a man sitting on a stool.

Another man kept the stalks of cane coming from the wagons that the farmers brought there from their fields. I was most interested in the old faithful horse that kept pulling the long shaft round and round. He'd worn a deep path in a circle from walking around and around.

The cane juice ran down a wooden trough into containers that emptied into an oblong vat. The vat or boiler was made of tin and reinforced with wooden strips and handles. When filled with cane juice, it was placed over a furnace. The molasses-maker furnace was made of stone, with a small chimney at one end, while the other end was open so that more wood could be added during the cooking process.

The length of time a run of juice should cook was determined by Mr. Beck, the expert molasses maker, who stood by with a long handle spoon. He stirred and skimmed off foam and tested it until the run was the right thickness. Then it was poured into barrels, and another run was started.

Dad and Mr. Beck gave me permission to sop the boiler after the last run. I sopped it first with a biscuit that my dad had brought for that purpose, then with my dirty fingers.

FARM LIFE WAS GOOD

Dad always said that there were two reliable guideposts for judging a farmer's wife and that was by her quilts and what she hung on her cloths-line. And the way to judge a farmer was by his wood pile and the looks of his team's harness.

Mama made all of our quilts; we had a surplus. She called some "Crazy Quilts" and some "Patchwork Quilts." She took pride in her quilts. Some had attractive and intricate designs, all were made from scraps.

Dad always had a big woodpile of maple and oak stacked between two trees. In another smaller stack he kept gray birch, poplar and split-up pine knots for a quick fire. Dad hauled the wood in a wagon and stacked it as high as he could reach. He was good with an ax.

Farm life was good.

I can still hear the music of hounds on a trail and the lonesome notes of a whippoorwill at dusk. I loved going barefooted and wearing overalls on my way to the river with a can of worms and a fishing pole in search of some high adventure fishing.

Farm life was good.

At sunset cows would come to the pasture gate to be milked, and we would call the chickens up from all around to be fed. I can still smell sweet watermelons in the fields after a summer rain and remember watching the rainbow with its many colors.

Farm life was good.

We picked blackberries in July and scuppernongs in September. I can still smell tobacco curing in the barns in early fall. We checked rabbit gums in the evening and rode to church in a buggy every Sunday.

Farm life was good.

When we all got together around the big fireplace in the cold of the winter, with all of our family, telling stories, roasting apples on a string, popping popcorn in a basket, roasting sweet potatoes in the ashes, and lots of laughter mixed in, farm life was good.

THE OLD FARM HOUSE

This old farm house, memories with many roots.
Now, only old apple trees bear fruit.

A post is covered with dead vines,
Giving evidence of the passing of time.
On it hangs a faded "NO TRESPASSING" sign,
A patchwork of vines, a haunting design.

Where are the flowers that use to grow?
Where are the box bushes of long ago?
I see no lilies blooming in a row.
They've been killed by the weeds, a mighty foe.

In this musky field I give a pause,
Beside a rusty pump, without a cause.
I see a chimney that seems in place,
Where a nest is holding a piece of lace.

A house with all its windows broken,

She's a lonely house with her door flung open.

A sagging front porch that's empty now.

Only a place where the rain drops down.

On the porch lies a shoe a lady once wore.

A house, a shoe, to be used no more.

Part of a welcome mat at the door,

I'm left with a feeling never felt before.

The wilted grass no longer green,

The neglect here is almost obscene.

Windows staring like hollow eyes,

Their purpose here has been denied.

Inside I see a mantel about to fall.

I see the paint flaking off the wall.

Wasp nests and spider webs dangling down,

A musty odor of dampness all around.

Floors all covered with grim and dust,
Once a proud stove now covered in rust.
A pile of trash never swept away,
Gathering more ugliness day-by-day.

From the wind, the tin roof cringes,
A loose door groans on its hinges.
A small breeze causes the house to sway,
Only a family of rats is willing to stay.
A broken padlock hangs on the door,
While termites eat away at the floor.

I hear loose boards painfully squeaking,
Making a sound like someone weeping.
This house secluded in all its gloom,
Making me feel I have intruded in a tomb.

A house never to be alive again,
I'm afraid it has reached its end.
It once was known as a strong home,

But the happy faces are now long gone.

It's now neglected and left to decay,
People forget when they are far away.
This place now brings only tears,
Its only joy is in memories of bygone years.

The vines prying the bricks apart
Are also at work on my broken heart.
I remember the happy games we played,
And friends that gathered to talk in the shade.

Abundant crops growing in the fields,
Happy children romping over the hills.
It's too late, I've done all I can.
How easy it would have been with a helping hand.
How little interest some seem to take.
What a difference working together would make.
When I grow old and no longer be,
I wonder what my old house will see.

THE OLD CEDAR BUCKET

On the farm, we had an old cedar water bucket sitting on a shelf on the little back porch. That bucket remained full of water from the nearby spring. Beside it sat our wash pan and a towel.

Inside the kitchen, we had a metal bucket on a washstand table with a metal dipper, but the cedar bucket on the back porch had a gourd dipper.

Right outside the kitchen door on a big tree, we had a large oak bucket hooked to a large nail. This was our slop bucket for the hogs. One day we saw a big, big snake with its head in the slop bucket. We tried to hit it with rocks, but the snake climbed up the tree out on a limb over the house. Somehow, we shook the limb and he fell off on the tin roof and slid down to the ground and Mama killed it with the hoe.

We had another old bucket that we carried to the fields where Dad was working for him to have a fresh drink. Water never tasted better than when dipped up by a gourd dipper from the brassbound old cedar bucket. It had a special aroma of freshness.

To me, the old cedar bucket out ranks the 'Old Oaken Bucket' of literary fame. Whether hanging suspended in a well or sitting on the back porch, it holds the best drink of water I've ever had. How I wish I had that old cedar Bucket, now.

OUR KITCHEN

Mother had white curtains at the kitchen windows. A corn shuck-scouring mop stood in a corner. That floor was almost white from being moped and scoured so often. Have you ever seen a shuck-scouring mop? It was an oblong board with holes augured through it. Clean, tough corn shucks were pulled tightly through each hole. It had a long handle. With plenty of elbow grease, it really could clean a floor.

Mother used a wood stove. I still yearn for her pies and cakes. We stored all of our dishes in a "pie safe." I still have that pie safe. Now 'aday' fancy electric gadgets cannot cook pies with the same old aroma and taste that the old wood stove did. I remember a pot hanging down in front of the fireplace where beans cooked.

On Saturday nights, we'd pop popcorn in a screen-like box with a handle on it over the open fire. In the winter, we would dress around the kitchen stove. Dad had his own coffee cup. He always poured his coffee into his saucer to cool, and then he'd drink from the saucer.

I miss the pies and chicken and dumplings, the green wood singing a happy tune, and us enjoying each other around the fireplace and wood stove.

THE OLD TOLL BRIDGE

The old toll bridge where I loved to go,

To hang over the side and watch the river flow.

Under the bridge, I found shelter from the rain.

It's where I first carved my name.

Here I spotted frogs with a flashlight.

It's where I saw a ghost one dark night.

The old toll bridge where I used to go,

It's gone now. I can no longer watch the river flow.

FAMILY PORTRAITS

There's the faces of my family in old frames.

I guess I'm the only one who still knows their names.

There's something about these old folks that I see

That makes me think they are watching over me.

In Grandpa's face, I see strength and a sense of fun.

There's my uncle, a brick mason, dark from the sun.

They are not with me now, but yet they are.

There's a connection of family from afar.

Now when I look I think I see

Just a little of their lives compressed in me.

NATURE

NIGHTS ARE BEAUTIFUL

Nighttime is beautiful, magical.

Look up above when the moon is full.

Its beauty can mean so much to you.

Adorable nightfall is a pleasant view.

I can see the glowing morning star,

And gaze at little ones dim and far.

The big dipper is shining bright in the sky,

Always shining bright until a new sunrise.

I'm gazing up at God's heavenly floor,

Through the haze, I see a crack in the door,

Giving a halo around His special star.

The one that led wise men from afar.

Here in the night waiting for sunrise,

The beauty of darkness is no surprise.

I've seen the horizon at evening sunset,

Where earth and sky meet and rest.

God arranged the stars high above,
God can change night to day with His love.
With reverence, I marvel at all of this.
Knowing beyond the sky is holy bliss.

May this feeling at twilight still
Be with me as I try to do His will.
Contented on this soft earthly sod,
 I feel the presence of almighty God.

Mel's Note: Nighttime is a time to think and meditate, pray and rest. I love the wee hours of night, just before dawn and the early mornings. God and nature feel at rest. I believe that Virgin Mary gave birth to Jesus early in the morning, between a beautiful sunset and a colorful sunrise.

CAMPING IN THE MOUNTAINS

Once I camped far up in the mountains.
Near a spring and a creek running by.
There was silence all around,
Except a hoot owl cry.

Here where tall oak trees loom,
And red mountain flowers bloom.
First morning snow on the ground.
I saw deer tracks all around.

Now a blazing fire from my wood pile,
To cook my food and keep warm by.
I've searched the rivers wide and far,
Slept in a boat many nights under the stars.
I've camped from mountain to sea,
But there's nothing like the mountains for me.

Across the state, I have roamed

But now I'm happy just being at home.

Now memories like warm embers glow.

My camping days are over, now I know.

CAMPING OUT

Camping out gives me a thrill,
With a fire to cook without a grill.
Where creatures are all about,
A wild rose and flowers are popping out.

A glowing campfire to dream by,
Roaring flames under open sky.
The sound of traffic now long gone,
I'm away from civilization all alone.

The morning comes so very slow,
The stars put on a delightful show.
Giving off beauty, shining bright.
Telling me, everything is all right.

Sleeping on the leaf covered ground,
With hoot owls and crickets all around.
I wake at sunrise feeling fresh,

No stress. I got enough rest.

With bacon frying, smelling so good,

I'd stay forever if I could.

I see morning glories drinking dew,

And a sky wearing an apron of blue.

Camping out, smelling a wood fire,

Relaxed and breathing good air,

Seeing a sunset and a sunrise,

Camping out is like winning a prize.

BEAUTY IN MY SIGHT

Everything is beautiful in my sight.
This old world can always be bright.
Flowers need not be in expensive vases.
True beauty can be found in many places.

Beauty is found in the colored hills,
And by a lake where the world stands still.
Beauty is in the mountains that climb so high,
Higher than the blue clouds as they float by.

I see the beautiful clouds that are colored blue.
God lifts one to let His face shine through.
Beauty is seeing little birds in their nest,
And knowing the master artist is at his best.

Beauty is on the beach of shifting sand,
Watching two lovers walking hand in hand.
God made this beauty and the ocean to roll.

It's up to us; he gave us a beautiful soul.

He gives hope every day and peace at night.

He made life beautiful in my sight.

BEAUTY EVERYWHERE

When happiness is so much desired,

And my routine is not inspired,

I won't sit around feeling blue.

God provides a much better view.

Even when health and wife are gone,

I can find happiness in my home.

No need to feel that life is bare,

If for others I care and share.

I look across my windowsill.

I see flowers budding on the hill,

All colored with beautiful birds.

Nature's songs are heard.

Being alone doesn't trouble me,

When white snow is on the tree.

There's much more beauty to see,

When my imagination can run free.

Even with the icy winters chill,
This beauty can give me a thrill.
With crumbs the birds I can feed.
With love, I care for their need.
I can show others that I care,
And enjoy breathing in the fresh air.

Even when the sky is dark I see
A warm fire is waiting for me.
On the mantle are many good books,
There's much to see, if I only look.

With icicles shimmering on the hill,
Little snowflakes can give me a thrill.
By this open fireplace, I can just be.
In my home, I am warm and free.

BY THE SEASHORE AT SUNRISE

I stand by the seashore all alone,

Watching the sunrise at early morn.

The horizon like a rose in colorful bloom,

The sea lights up, erasing the gloom.

On this deserted beach of sand,

Only my tracks are on this barren land.

A gleam of light, darkness is gone,

On the edge of night, now it's dawn.

Here by the water's edge, in the foam,

I'm watching the shadows moving on.

My mind and thoughts are now set free,

To ponder the mysteries of the sea.

My imagination controls my thoughts,

As I check to see what the tide has brought.

I hear a sea gull flapping its wings.

I'm lost in thought, but I hear many things.

The wind blows softly, the morning is here.
The sparkling sunrise now appears,
Leaving a feeling of freedom on the shore.
Yes, another sunrise it's mine once more.

I walk from the surf leaving no trace.
The incoming tide, my tracks will erase.
By this great ocean, I watch and dream,
Knowing God is a mighty power supreme.

"If I take the wings of the morning, and dwell in the uttermost parts of the sea; even there shall Thy hand lead me, and Thy right hand shall hold me." – Psalm 139:9-10

Mel's Note: I was a beachcomber at Carolina Beach for most of my life. I remember the first time each of my sons saw the ocean. We were excited after driving 200 miles. There it lay in the bright sun light. The ocean and the sandy beach, how could I tell my small sons about the great, ancient sea. There is no way. We took off our shoes, and I took their hands, shivering with excitement, and we ran to the sea.

Many years later, I stood alone by the seaside, gazing out across the sea I felt as free as I had ever felt. I let my imagination and dreams take over. But my thoughts returned to my family. "This can only be good when shared with them," I thought.

ANOTHER SUNRISE

Sunrise is the greatest time of the day. I've seen the sun rise from the mountains to the sea. I've seen many sunrises camping with my Boy Scout Troop while building a fire to cook our breakfast.

I've seen the sun rise from the top of the Blue Ridge Mountains, rom the Outer Banks shores, and from a ship at sea. The best sunrises were with Martha on the Carolina beaches fishing and at Fort Caswell with friends from the First Baptist Church.

Now I'm watching it all alone except for the birds singing their glorious songs and the beautiful colors of azaleas and roses that Martha planted.

From my front porch, I'm thinking of the sunrise the morning of Jesus' resurrection. And thinking about Mary Magdalene coming to the tomb, while it was still dark but at sunrise saw Jesus. John describes her revelation as occurring, "just as the day was breaking."

Yes, it is good to see the darkness disappearing and another beautiful sunrise. I think of God's light that shines in the darkness. We have no fear when we are in God's light.

DOWN THE YADKIN

Shoving off into water so deep,

In the bottom of my boat I fell asleep.

The night passed, I'm awake early,

Waiting for the fog, to see more clearly.

Then a streak of light from sunbeams,

Time to continue my journey of dreams.

I smell honeysuckles, no longer dark.

A place to remember, sad to embark.

The rumbling water was mirror clear.

Now the lonesome shadows disappear.

I see the hump of a turtle very near.

He knows no danger, he has no fear.

I use my Scout shirt for a sail,

Catching a strong wind, away I sail.

I pass enchanted islands down the river,

Places I could live contented forever.

Now more rapids I must face,

Just ahead another dangerous place.

I guide my canoe through circles of foam,

Now I am thinking of home sweet home.

My muscles are aching more and more,

As I move close to the root filled shore.

Close by a snake makes the water quiver,

I'm cold with fear, I start to shiver.

With blisters on both of my hands,

I have too much pride to take to land.

Even when clouds bring on more rain,

I paddle on not making much gain.

I keep close to land as I slowly creep,

To be safe if I sank while in my sleep.

I open my eyes to early morn,

I hear the geese like a bugle-horn.

A spider web in front of my boat,

With little white letters a spider wrote,

I think it said, "Keep on, keep on."

I gained new hope, some soreness gone.

Mother Nature said with her living truth,

"You can do it, son, you have your youth."

Stronger now than when the journey begun,

Now tan and dark from the boiling sun,

Leaving the riverbanks covered with trees,

Entering our home dock that I can see.

I shout with joy and jump up high,

I've reached my goal under a happy sky.

WINTER'S ART

From my front porch on a snowy night,
I see dancing snowflakes in flight.
Snow on rose bushes making them white,
Ice covering trees shining bright.

My heart is filled with sheer delight,
As the dark earth vanishes out of sight.
A beautiful sight, snow covering the ground
and meadows but not making a sound.

Snow in the moonlight, what a delight.
I hug my lover up tight.
This winter's art so snowy and white,
By morning piled high, a magical sight.

Even the wind stopped to see,
The heavy winter trees.
The crystal-glisten of the leafless host,

As the sun gleams on winter's ghost.

All this so pure and white it seems,

Like the artist painted a wintery dream.

Winter's art is a beautiful sight.

The greatest artist painted this magical white.

WINTER WONDERLAND

Abundant harvest, then winter intervenes,

With drifting snow covering the scene.

With fearful force, it changes the weather.

Yet, winter is a source of many pleasures.

When flowers sadly leave the green hollows,

Soon tiny snowflakes will gently follow.

Oceans of snowdrifts will cover the scene

Only showing the hue of the evergreen.

Ice castles are made from the morning dew.

Underneath, fresh life can soon start anew.

Beneath an old slab pile of rot and decay,

Nature's small creatures find a hideaway.

On a limb, a bird nest brown and bare,

Only the wind breaks the silence there.

Trees disrobe, scattering leaves about,

Laying them to rest on a winter's couch.

In fields, you'll see only a faded flower,
They will bloom again with a mystic power.
Now they are buried in the snow so deep,
They are only waiting to wake from sleep.

Everywhere the sparkling snow is spread,
Behind me my big deep footprints tread.
Glistening snow covers all the trees,
Frozen icicles as far as eyes can see.

With the white earth reflecting a luster,
And the crimson clouds all in a cluster.
The nippy cool breeze my face does caress,
The bright colored sunset I love the best.

White covered peaks are there to greet,
And the frozen creek is a good place to meet.
Here we can skate across the ice at will,

Even race with sleds down a steep hill.

We can make a snowman, fat and straight,
And have a snowball fight till very late.
In winter our bad memories can drop away,
In this wonderland, how can we go astray?
For under the snow life will soon resume,
Plants and roses will soon re-bloom.

A TIME FOR ROAMING

When I was a child I could dream all day.
I'd go deep into the woods and get far away.
Where troubles and trials are far and few.
My young life was good and all things new.
Youth is for carefree living, I do agree,
A time for roaming, like a river flowing free.
An age for learning with a yearning in my heart,
Life's an adventure, a mystery and I'm a part.

At sunrise, I wander down to my favorite spot,
Down a steep hill to the big rock.
I lay on its top dreaming and make-believe.
Looking up, I see the sky through birch leaves.
I'm living in a world of magic, happy as can be.
Knowing the big oak trees are watching over me.
Here I have no fears, I feel save for a while.
With the sun shining into the heart of a child.

The blue clouds are drifting and rolling above,

Nature's beauty, giving a feeling of peace and love.

I feel her strength as her arms embrace me.

With hugs from branches of a weeping willow tree.

A dream world I enter with wonder and new sight.

Overhead a blue bird flaps its wings in flight.

In a bush a rusty brown thrush builds a nest.

Loud is the chirp of crickets, disturbing my rest.

Hearing the flow of water rippling over a stone,

I see the beauty of a proud butterfly. I'm not alone.

I skip a rock across the water, the silence is broken.

From the swamp a catbird screams, a warning is spoken.

Echoes from the catbird's call, lingers over the stream.

While flowers nod to me and me to them as in a dream.

Nearby many birds come to feast in a mulberry tree.

They share with squirrels, they are all free.

Down the river, I sail a ship made from birch bark.

In the distance, I hear the song of a meadowlark.

I follow the ship downstream around the big rock.

For more boats, I use driftwood and pine bark.

Here on the big rock it's like a colored picture book.

I see the green forest and a clear shady brook.

From the earth a spring, like a fountain flows.

Here spring lizards, crawfish, and tadpoles grow.

AFTER THE STORM

I watched God wash the world last night;

His sweet shower on high.

When the morning came, he hung it out to dry.

Every blade of grass and every trembling tree,

He flung showers against the hills, swept the mighty sea.

God washed the world last night; wish he'd washed me,

All clean of my dust and dirt, just like that old birch tree.

If times are hard, and you feel blue,

Think of the others worrying too.

Just because your trials are many,

Don't think the rest of us haven't any.

Life is made up of smiles and tears,

Joys and sorrows mixed with fears.

And though to us it seems one-sided,

Troubles are pretty well divided.

If you could look in every heart,

You'd find that each one has a hurt part.

Those who travel fortune's road,

Sometimes carry the biggest load.

2017 NEW YEAR'S MESSAGE

As the final days of 2016 fade away into memory and history I can look back at one of the worst physical years of my 99-year-life. Yet, I can also look back and see that I have grown spiritually.

I can look back in gratitude for all that God has done in my life and in my family's life. I am so thankful. I am sad for the loved ones lost. Life's journey is a combination of joy and sorrow, gain and loss, good days and bad days.

With the coming of a new year, spend time with your loved ones. Make good memories for the future. Reflect on the wonderful moments of the past year. Forget the bad moments.

Place great importance on your personal and spiritual growth. Keep growing in faith and seeking out new ways to serve God and others. Use your faith and values in your daily life. Attend weekly church services and continue to study the Bible.

I'm looking forward to 2017. What a blessing to be living at the start of a New Year, my 100th. My prayer is that next New Year Day I'll be sending out a New Year's Message again to each of you.

Editor's Note

Mel left this earth on May 22, 2017.

Release of the book was planned for the July 16, 2017 celebration of Mel's 100th birthday. As only God could arrange, we finished ahead of schedule. Mel read the entire proof while waiting in the Baptist Hospital emergency room on May 17.

I had the honor to be with him in the hospital just before his transport to Hospice of Davidson County. There was a special feeling in the room that night. I could almost see the impatient white horses harnessed to his chariot of fire, anxious to get one of the giants home. Literally thousands awaited Mel's homecoming, especially Martha and their daughter.

Mel embodied faith. He's left encouragement for you and me in this book. He awaits the day when we'll join him on a front porch to sit a spell.

Melvin C. Young Sr.

1941

2017

To order copies of this book or share a Mel story:

Carla Harper

P.O. 39436

Greensboro, NC 27438

www.carlagharper.com/mel-young/

www.ingramcontent.com/pod-product-compliance
Lightning Source LLC
Chambersburg PA
CBHW020610300426
44113CB00007B/585